Cambridge Opera Handbooks

CW00392167

Richard Strauss
Arabella

CAMBRIDGE OPERA HANDBOOKS

This is a series of studies of individual operas written for the opera-goer or record-collector as well as the student or scholar. Each volume has three main concerns: historical, analytical and interpretative. There is a detailed description of the genesis of each work, the collaboration between librettist and composer, and the first performance and subsequent stage history. A full synopsis considers the opera as a structure of musical and dramatic effects, and there is also a musical analysis of a section of the score. The analysis, like the history, shades naturally into interpretation: by a careful combination of new essays and excerpts from classic statements the editors of the handbooks show how critical writing about the opera, like the production and performance, can direct or distort appreciation of its structural elements. A final section of documents gives a select bibliography, a discography, and guides to other sources. Each book is published in hard covers and as a paperback.

Published titles

Richard Wagner: *Parsifal* by Lucy Beckett
W. A. Mozart: *Don Giovanni* by Julian Rushton
C. W. von Gluck: *Orfeo* by Patricia Howard
Igor Stravinsky: *The Rake's Progress* by Paul Griffiths
Leoš Janáček: *Kát'a Kabanová* by John Tyrrell
Giuseppe Verdi: *Falstaff* by James A. Hepokoski
Benjamin Britten: *Peter Grimes* by Philip Brett
Giacomo Puccini: *Tosca* by Mosco Carner
Benjamin Britten: *The Turn of the Screw* by Patricia Howard
Richard Strauss: *Der Rosenkavalier* by Alan Jefferson
Claudio Monteverdi: *Orfeo* by John Whenham
Giacomo Puccini: *La bohème* by Arthur Groos and Roger Parker
Giuseppe Verdi: *Otello* by James A. Hepokoski
Benjamin Britten: *Death in Venice* by Donald Mitchell
W. A. Mozart: *Le nozze di Figaro* by Tim Carter
W. A. Mozart: *Die Entführung aus dem Serail* by Thomas Bauman
Hector Berlioz: *Les Troyens* by Ian Kemp
Alban Berg: *Wozzeck* by Douglas Jarman
Claude Debussy: *Pelléas et Mélisande* by Roger Nichols and Richard Langham Smith

Richard Strauss
Arabella

KENNETH BIRKIN

*The right of the
University of Cambridge
to print and sell
all manner of books
was granted by
Henry VIII in 1534.
The University has printed
and published continuously
since 1584.*

CAMBRIDGE UNIVERSITY PRESS

Cambridge
New York   New Rochelle   Melbourne   Sydney

Published by the Press Syndicate of the University of Cambridge
The Pitt Building, Trumpington Street, Cambridge CB2 1RP
40 West 20th Street, New York, NY 10011, USA
10 Stamford Road, Oakleigh, Melbourne 3166, Australia

First published 1989

Printed in Great Britain at the University Press, Cambridge

British Library cataloguing in publication data

Birkin, Kenneth
Richard Strauss: Arabella. – (Cambridge
opera handbooks).
1. Opera in German. Strauss, Richard,
1865–1949. Arabella
I. Title
782.1′092′4

Library of Congress cataloguing in publication data

Birkin, Kenneth.
Richard Strauss, Arabella / Kenneth Birkin.
    p. cm. – (Cambridge opera handbooks)
Bibliography: p.
Includes index.
ISBN 0 521 34031 4. ISBN 0 521 33577 9 (pbk.)
1. Strauss, Richard, 1864–1949. Arabella. I. Title.
II. Series.
ML410.S93B5 1989
782.1′092′4 – dc19   88–29953 CIP

ISBN 0 521 34031 4 hard covers
ISBN 0 521 33577 9 paperback

ME

For Louise, Emma, Lucy and Nicholas

Contents

Illustrations

I am grateful to the following for permission to reproduce illustrations: Theatermuseum, Cologne (Plate 1); Österreichische National-bibliothek, Vienna (Plates 2, 10, 11, 12, 13, 14); Hungarian State Opera, Budapest (Plates 3, 4, 5, 6); Dr Dietrich Roller and the *Theatersammlung* of the Österreichische Nationalbibliothek (Plates 7, 8); Frau Alice Strauss and the *Musiksammlung* of the Öster-reichische Nationalbibliothek (Plates 9a and b).

Acknowledgements

Strauss scholars owe a great debt to the late Dr Willi Schuh of Zurich, to whom I would like to pay my own posthumous tribute – especially for his personal encouragement of my work over the last few years. Space forbids mention of many others who have contributed to my efforts, but I would like to record my gratitude to Dr Günter Brosche and his staff at the *Musiksammlung* of the Österreichische Nationalbibliothek in Vienna for so much friendly and practical assistance, and for permission to quote from the unpublished Strauss and Fanto letters in their care. I would also like to thank Frau Alice Strauss for allowing me to include two facsimile pages from the Act 3 *Arabella* sketchbook; Dr Dietrich Roller for use of the sketches made by his father for the Viennese premiere of the opera; the Archive of the Hungarian National Opera in Budapest, who generously granted permission for the inclusion of the Oláh costume sketches of 1935; and the Theatermuseum of the University of Cologne, who provided the Ursuleac photograph for the frontispiece of the book. Thanks are also due to Professor Otto Strasser, Dr Clemens Hellsberg (Vienna Philharmonic Archive), Dr Götz-Klaus Kende (Clemens Krauss Archive) and to Dr Porzsolt (Regensburg), each of whom answered my queries with patience and promptitude. Similarly, thanks are due to the staffs of the *Theatersammlung* and the *Bildsammlung* of the Österreichische Nationalbibliothek in Vienna; the archive of the Semperoper, Dresden; Birmingham University Library; Birmingham Central Reference Library and the British Library Sound Archive. I would like to thank Penny Souster at Cambridge University Press for her patience and courtesy; Maren Coleman for so readily advising on points of translation and Donald Forrest Johnstone (Richmond), from whose meticulous reading of the manuscript and from whose erudite comments I have reaped inestimable benefit. Quotations from the Strauss/Hofmannsthal correspondence are taken from the Hammelmann and Osers edition (Collins, 1961); all other translations are my own, unless otherwise acknowledged in the text or notes. I send greetings to Frau Luise Gregor, and to all my Viennese friends; their support has been a profound source of encouragement over the years. Finally I salute Frau Gertrude Leberl of Regensburg, whose labours on behalf of this book, being inexhaustible, can be neither measured nor adequately repaid.

Arabella
Op. 79

Lyrical comedy in three acts

Dramatis personae

Count Waldner, retired cavalry officer	Bass
Adelaide, his wife	Mezzo-soprano
Arabella ⎫ their daughters	Soprano
Zdenka ⎭	Soprano
Matteo, a military officer	Tenor
Mandryka, a Croatian landowner	Baritone
Count Elemer ⎫	Tenor
Count Dominik ⎬ Arabella's suitors	Baritone
Count Lamoral ⎭	Bass
Fiakermilli	Coloratura soprano
Fortune-teller	Soprano
Welko, Mandryka's bodyguard	
Djura ⎫ Mandryka's servants	
Jankel ⎭	
Room Waiter	
Arabella's Companion	
Three card players	
Doctor, Groom, Coachmen, Ball Guests, Waiters	

Vienna, 1860

Abbreviations

Rehearsal figures in the full score are referred to in the text as 'Fig. 100', etc.; numbers in smaller type following them indicate bar numbers computed from those figures. These references may be supplemented by the relevant page numbers from the vocal score:

Fig. 108^3–110^7, v.s. pp. 331–2

In the notes, the Strauss/Hofmannsthal *Correspondence*, trans. H. Hammelmann and E. Osers (Collins, London 1961), is referred to simply as *Correspondence*; the author of the letter is identified by a bracketed initial.

1   Viorica Ursuleac at the end of Act 1 (*Mein Elemer*): world premiere, Dresden, October 1933

1 *Strauss and Hofmannsthal: the collaborative background*

Arabella is the valedictory opus in the Strauss/Hofmannsthal operatic canon. As the fulfilment of a recognisable collaborative goal, it provides a platform from which to survey the long and fruitful creative partnership which engendered it. It was in October 1903, while Strauss was composing *Salome*, that Hofmannsthal's verse drama based on Sophocles's *Elektra* opened at the Kleines Theater in Berlin under the direction of Max Reinhardt. Already aware of the poet's interest in his work, Strauss was quick to recognise the musical potential of so powerfully expressed and dramatic a concept.

Indeed, some three years before, Hofmannsthal had approached the composer with a ballet sketch; but despite its obvious merits, it had been politely set aside in favour of more pressing commitments. Now, two operas later, stimulated by Reinhardt's production, and with *Salome* well on the way towards completion, Strauss acted promptly, formulating a proposal which evoked an eager response from the poet, who replied, 'It is, I must say, the hope of no mean pleasure which you have aroused in me. Will you let me know in a few lines whether this hope may remain alive or is to be buried.'[1] Strauss's reply was equally enthusiastic: 'I would ask you urgently to give me first refusal with anything composable that you write. Your manner has so much in common with mine; we were born for one another and are certain to do fine things together if you remain faithful to me.'[2] This set the seal on a collaboration unique in opera. During two decades this remarkable creative venture saw the completion of nine full-scale works for the musical stage; and the preservation of their working correspondence during the entire period gives a rare glimpse behind the creative scenes. Described by Edward Sackville-West as 'One of the most detailed records ever preserved of the creative imagination at work on its materials',[3] these letters remain a fundamental source for all Strauss scholars.

Until the composition of *Salome*, completed in 1905, Strauss's

1

reputation, despite the *succès d'estime* of *Guntram* and *Feuersnot*, rested upon his tone poems, which had progressed as far as the *Sinfonia Domestica*. To some extent the single-act *Salome* – highly illustrative in musical effect and employing an orchestrally motivated symphonic design – constitutes a stage projection of this evocatively powerful medium. Strauss saw *Elektra* as a logical extension of the *Salome* 'line' and there is evidence that Hofmannsthal himself had been influenced by Wilde's play in the shaping of his text. The notorious success of *Elektra*, which utilised flagrantly expressionist musical devices to interpret the psychological conflicts of the drama, confirmed Strauss's avant-garde position in the eyes of his contemporaries. Once committed to Hofmannsthal, however, his horizons broadened, as the poet, assuming the role of 'cultural arbiter', propelled him in a largely unforeseen direction, encouraging Strauss to adopt his own, admittedly somewhat rarefied, aestheticism and to turn his back upon the Wagnerian heritage, which remained nevertheless an inspiration.

The path from *Elektra* to *Arabella* was unpredictable to Strauss's peers, and remains obscure to some observers today. The perceived alteration of style which produced the romantic 'classicism' of *Der Rosenkavalier* has been called 'regressive' – by implication, an opting out – a symptom of artistic complacency. Nevertheless, whatever was lost by abrogation of the *Elektra* vein, posterity has benefited uniquely from the collaborators' theatrical experiments of the 1920s and 30s, manifest in the search for a new rationality of means, form and expression. This emerged as an attempt to establish a working balance between the musical, literary, visual and psychological elements of the drama. The ultimate achievement, despite the curtailment brought about by Hofmannsthal's tragic death in 1929, was substantial.

Arabella, the last major project to be completed by the poet, stands at the end of an astonishingly varied yet coherent series of musical stage works. Both artists were conscious of having stumbled on a project identifiable with the goal of 'collaborative theatre' towards which they believed themselves to be progressing. As such it has a significant position in the Strauss/Hofmannsthal operatic canon.

Hofmannsthal was born in 1874 and spent most of his life in or near Vienna, the city with which he is so closely identified. His precocity revealed itself in the accomplished poetic lyricism of the 1890s; this, together with the early verse dramas, attracted admiration from his contemporaries and formed the basis of a European reputation. This promising beginning was interrupted by an artistic crisis publicly expressed in the *Letter to Lord Chandos* (1902), which revealed the poet's loss of faith in the ability of the written word to express the complex, underlying mysticism of his ideas. Disillusioned, he forsook purely poetic forms and turned towards the theatre – adding a new expressive dimension which enabled him to reach out to a wider public.

The early works with their evocative but often obscure symbolism conveyed an obsession with the concept of *Prae-existenz*, which contrasts the transient quality of life with the higher realities before birth and after death. A recurrent (although often submerged) *motif* in Hofmannsthal's thought, this 'theme', discernible in *Ariadne auf Naxos* and *Die Frau ohne Schatten*, is linked to the other recurrent notion of 'transformation', a phenomenon inherent in the 'meeting' or 'encounter' which constitutes an experience of spiritual receptivity, where emotional uncertainty is big with the prospect of change.

Methinks it is not the embrace but the encounter which is the decisive erotic dalliance. There is no other moment when the sensual is so soulful, the soulful so sensual: here all is flux, all unattached. . .A greeting is something boundless. This somewhere, this uncertain and yet passionately hoping desire, this calling of the unknown to her that is unknown is what is so potent. It belongs to a higher order of thing by which the stars are moved and by which thoughts generate one another.[4]

In Hofmannsthal's hands, the concept turns out to be of pivotal importance – not only in his stage comedies *Der Schwierige* and *Der Unbestechliche*, but also, in the operas, at such moments as the 'recognition' scene in *Elektra*, the first meeting of Sophie and Octavian in *Der Rosenkavalier*, the *Ariadne* finale and in the anticipations, encounters and final trystings of *Arabella*.

As an Austrian and a Viennese, Hofmannsthal inevitably recognised the historical, cultural and spiritual heritage of generations of Habsburg rule. The decline of the Austrian State and the outbreak of the First World War aroused in him strong patriotic feelings which found expression in a series of historical essays written from 1915 onwards. Originally conceived in lecture form,[5] they were a deliberate attempt to recreate the 'Austrian Myth'. His aim was a revival of those spiritual qualities peculiar to his homeland, as an antidote to materialism and a contribution to the restructuring of a viable postwar Europe. He also sought to propagate his ideas and ideals through the symbolic ritual of the theatre. One perceives a new significance in his approach to religious allegory, with its popular appeal to large audiences. The morality plays, *Das große Welttheater* and *Jedermann*, both hugely successful, became over the years an institution at the Salzburg Festival founded by Hofmannsthal, Strauss and Reinhardt in 1922. Typically, in the festival manifesto of 1921, Hofmannsthal writes:

The introduction of musical/theatrical festivals at Salzburg means breathing new life into that which was once alive, giving encouragement to the original life-impetus of this Bavarian-Austrian race, and helping its people to find their way back to a true spiritual expression.[6]

The last stage in this process of artistic synthesis and cultural dissemination was inevitably found in opera, with its formal combination of musical and theatrical elements. Hofmannsthal's decision to collaborate with Strauss was not an interesting diversionary experiment in a literary career, but the first step in pursuit of a deliberate and clearly envisaged socio-political and cultural goal. For Hofmannsthal, as for Strauss, opera became a celebratory act, a festive occasion: the ultimate cultural phenomenon.

Naturally, that summary view of Hofmannsthal's artistic development does less than justice to the subtlety of his achievement or to the complexity of the personality which his work reflects. There is evidence that Strauss encountered serious difficulties in his attempts to grapple with the abstract and often esoteric ideas to which his librettist was attached. The factor which had attracted him to the poet, and which sustained him despite misunderstandings, was his recognition of the underlying musical nature of Hofmannsthal's lyric gift – nothing could threaten a working relationship which held so much promise and which provided so powerful a musical stimulus.

The attributes which Strauss, as the foremost composer of his day, brought to the collaboration included an unparalleled technical accomplishment, supplemented by a disconcerting objectivity of expression – the result of his intellectual powers. An understanding of the course of Western music, gained through his experience as a conductor in the concert hall and opera house, facilitated an assessment of his own contribution to that development from the standpoint of a perceived historical tradition. His awareness of this tradition was constantly being expanded by a variety of cultural pursuits, including a self-imposed and widely based programme of reading.

The prospect of collaboration with Hofmannsthal was undoubtedly attractive to one whose work as an operatic composer was dominated by the relationship between words and music. 'The battle between words and music has been the problem of my life from the beginning',[7] he asserted in later years. Certainly, a creative association with such a writer as Hofmannsthal presented an intellectual and artistic challenge of the highest order. The aim, from the beginning, 'That of two artists who, with imagination and delicacy, are seeking new ways of expression',[8] found its most characteristic realisation in the declamatory nature and pace of works such as *Ariadne, Intermezzo*, and *Arabella*, whose theatrical effect was dependent upon the comprehensibility of the dialogue. All the composer's skill and artistry is directed towards this end; its achievement takes account of practical elements ranging from the definition of vocal tessitura and pitch to the precise computation of accompanying instrumental forces. Complementary factors – action, decor, costume, lighting and production techniques – are no less important, all being closely monitored by poet and composer prior to performance. Such practical awareness suggests that Strauss the musician, through his understanding of the theatre, approaches the status of the dramatist; while Hofmannsthal the dramatist, through his ability to summon up an evocative language of sound, approaches that of the musician – a truism, but it contributed importantly to the success of the collaboration.

In spite of a mutual acknowledgement of the significance of their partnership, and despite their determination to preserve their separate artistic personalities – 'A reliance on complete respect and consideration for each other's share in the work, without which a collaboration such as ours would break down at once'[9] – one recognises, from time to time, a certain superiority in Hofmannsthal's attitude, deep-rooted in his class and upbringing; an unspoken prejudice against Strauss's 'bourgeois' Bavarian background, which he profoundly mistrusted. His efforts to regulate the artistic pulse of the collaboration, while generally benign and often salutary, on occasion led the composer into areas of psychological unintelligibility from which his partner was powerless to rescue him. Naturally, over the years, so intense a commitment between two such individual spirits generated tensions and misunderstandings. It is a mark of their mutual respect that each was, ultimately, able to respond to the criticism of the other. Indeed, such strictures, by virtue of the intellectual exchanges they provoked, were turned to good effect.

Perhaps after all, one of Hofmannsthal's most important contributions to the collaborative venture was to face the composer with a new aesthetic dimension; with a new conceptual goal beyond his previous envisaging. Perhaps too, it was in Strauss's efforts to rise to the artistic challenge presented by the poet that the real value of the partnership lay. In the cut and thrust of argument, Strauss found a stimulus which aroused him from the complacency inherent in his richly endowed and prolific musical nature.

Strauss in turn placed his practical theatrical knowledge at Hofmannsthal's disposal, supplying the needed formal and dramatic expertise, and labouring clear-sightedly to steer him away from the pitfalls into which his idealistic nature led him. The composer – a realist about opera and the stage – knew that effective theatre depended upon 'flesh and blood' situations. He understood the practical requirements of popular success; and Hofmannsthal's tendency to cloak his ideas in symbolic obscurity was called into question. Scenes were recast, and ploys introduced at the instigation of the composer, which, although not always welcomed by his partner, once adopted were seen to be right. One famous instance of dramatic restructuring occurs in the second-act *finale* of *Rosenkavalier*, but later, a similar problem arose in *Arabella* which provoked Strauss to remark

It seems to me that we've reached the same point as at that time in Act II of *Rosenkavalier*, – you then trusted my dramatic instinct to give the action its decisive impulse – you admit yourself that you approach the ultimate dramatic consequences with invariable hesitation – and I believe we have here another case in point. Act I is good. . . and could pass as a mere exposition. But Act II must be invested with conflicts and tensions, of which it is now entirely devoid – the whole thing is a mere lyrical gurgling – so that a real explosion in Act III is felt as a satisfactory solution.[10]

The composer's position is unassailable; his conclusions demonstrate clearly the diverse – but complementary – nature of the partners' talents. Indeed, both Hofmannsthal's idealism and Strauss's down-to-earth objectivity had a role to play in establishing the dramatic viability of their collaborative work. Despite warm exchange, altercation and argument, a balance was struck between the 'ideal' and the 'practical', poet and composer, words and music.

The stylistic change after *Elektra* is expressed by the establishment in *Der Rosenkavalier* of an apparently 'classical' format which provides for 'set pieces' in the traditional manner. The fluid rhythm of the text enables the lyrical moments of the score, marked by solo and ensemble 'numbers', to emerge naturally from the recitative-like 'conversational' medium. This conception, employing the motivic power of a large orchestra, introduced to the operatic stage a subtlety of expression akin to the spoken drama. The prime mover in this spiritual and stylistic integration of traditional and modern techniques was Hofmannsthal, who explained,

We must get entirely clear between us the style in which you intend to write this opera. If I rightly understand the hints you threw out and which struck me as being extremely promising, you intend to create something altogether novel in style, something which (since every development in the arts proceeds in cycles) will resemble more closely the older type of opera rather than *Meistersinger* or *Feuersnot*. You intend, unless I wholly misunderstood your hints, to alternate set numbers with passages which approximate to the old *secco* recitative.[11]

This 'something novel' proved to be a conceptual equality of 'words' and 'music' from which developed that inflected *parlando* manner so crucial to the stage success of *Rosenkavalier*, and which was to reach even greater expressive flexibility in *Arabella* some twenty years later.

After two serious works, *Salome* and *Elektra*, Strauss was ready to explore a lighter, happier, more operetta-like vein. The eighteenth-century setting and obvious *Figaro* parallels of *Rosenkavalier* were ideally suited to his needs, although they also encouraged him to reflect a musical classicism which disorientated the critics as much as it delighted the opera-going public. *Der Rosenkavalier*, therefore, represents a decided change of direction, which, while it disconcerted 'informed' opinion, can be rationalised in the light of an early remark by Strauss, that each of his operas sets out to resolve specific problems posed by its dramatic substance, *milieu* and textual format. Although to his contemporaries Strauss appeared very much 'out of line' with his traditionally conceived *Komödie für Musik*, it would be mistaken to measure his achievements against those of his contemporaries using 'serial' and atonal techniques. For both Strauss and Hofmannsthal, progress is defined as the refinement of expressive resource in a gradual development towards an elemental unity of 'words' and 'music' as a means of serving the drama: a development in nature rather than in kind. The way forward was certainly not without pitfalls and often, as one sees in *Ariadne*, success was wrested from apparent failure. It was nevertheless in direct response to the admitted *longueurs* of *Die Frau ohne Schatten* and *Die ägyptische Helena* that *Intermezzo* and *Arabella* were born.

Ariadne auf Naxos (1912) marks a step in the development which, after *Arabella*, reached its peak thirty years later in the Strauss/ Krauss-inspired *Capriccio*. A combination of play and opera, Hofmannsthal's original concept of *Ariadne* proved intractable, appealing neither to the 'straight' theatre nor to the music-loving public. But as an attempt to integrate ballet, pantomime, speech, music, comedy and tragedy, and as an expression of 'intimate' theatre, it indicated the direction in which Strauss and Hofmannsthal were travelling. Inevitably, and in due course, this musically garnished version of Molière's *Le bourgeois gentilhomme*, went its own way, but its baroque format stimulated Strauss to experiment with reduced instrumental forces, contributing one solution to the perennial problem of balance between pit and stage through the formulation of a neo-classical style.

Musically, *Ariadne* represents a real gain – although it provided a severe test for the collaborators as they struggled to define, not for the first or the last time, the extent of their artistic freedoms within the collaborative environment. It was the composer's misgivings in the face of Hofmannsthal's *penchant* for symbolism that proved the most serious stumbling-block. But their painfully established mutual right to 'freedom of speech' inside the 'workshop' moved Strauss, who saw the danger of incomprehensibility, to confide

The piece did not fully convince me until after I had read your letter, which is so beautiful and explains the meaning of the action so wonderfully that a superficial musician like myself could not, of course have tumbled to it. But isn't this a little dangerous? And isn't some of the interpretation still lacking in the action itself? If even I couldn't see it, just think of the audience and the critics.[12]

These remarks prompted Hofmannsthal to supply a new 'Prose scene which is to precede the opera', an idea Strauss welcomed since it would 'Explain and motivate the whole action'. This development was of the highest importance, giving rise eventually to the *Ariadne Vorspiel* of 1917. This by-passing of the Molière play brought about a refinement of the *Rosenkavalier parlando* which was to have far-reaching effects in the future. Both partners recognised the significance of their achievement in this new version of the work. 'In the first act of *Ariadne*, I effected, with absolute security, alternation between pure prose, *secco* and accompanied recitative, a device which I have now brought to its ultimate conclusion in *Intermezzo*',[13] Strauss explained much later; and Hofmannsthal wrote with equal satisfaction:

It does me good to think that I, who hardly consider myself as standing even at the extreme periphery of your art, should have found – with that instinct which is the common bond between all creative artists, over the heads, so to speak, of the rest of the crowd – the right thing to do in producing this particular work which literally forced upon you a definite style, only to give you back your freedom more fully on a higher plane.[14]

While the resolution of the problems that beset *Ariadne* ultimately yielded a way forward and a new approach, its successor, *Die Frau ohne Schatten*, could not benefit from the stylistic and technical solutions so far achieved. Apart from the interruption and chaos caused by the outbreak of World War I, composition was hindered by a plot so unintelligible that Hofmannsthal was forced into a written justification of its symbolism in the form of a vastly expanded prose version – the *Erzählung*. In pure self-defence, Strauss fell back upon his Wagnerian inheritance, creating music drama on a grand scale. The gestation of this high-minded *opera seria* extended over some five years, and during its composition Strauss sought relief in lighter tasks. These included the *Ariadne Vorspiel* (1916/17), and *Intermezzo*, begun in 1918, completed in 1923, and using his own text.

This *bürgerliche Komödie* is the third significant step along the road to *Arabella*. Based on an incident in the composer's private life, it demonstrates the new technical paths which he was following. *Intermezzo* represents a landmark in modern opera, cutting across the division of the acts with a series of swiftly changing cinematographically-inspired scenes based on a natural conversationally-paced dialogue. Hofmannsthal never really came to terms with this work, a 'bourgeois comedy'[15] whose subject caused him extreme embarrassment. But he was quick to recognise the scope and pedigree of his friend's achievement, pointing out,

You have striven here for a new style (starting from what is suggested in the *Ariadne Vorspiel* and to some extent also of course from *Rosenkavalier*), and you have achieved what you wanted. That is very much. . . Certain features of what you have now done can in future be relied upon as vested and indefeasible qualities. This is the real point of artistic development and in this sense one can speak of a master, indeed a master above all, learning and growing through what he has learnt.[16]

Whatever Hofmannsthal himself had learnt from *Intermezzo* – and the evidence suggests that he took account of its epigrammatic, 'telegram style', and 'looser, dissolved', scenic form – it was too late to benefit *Die ägyptische Helena*. By the time the letter above was written, the entire text of the opera and the music of the first act were almost complete, and its highly symbolic, allegorical style irrevocably fixed. The swift-footed *Intermezzo* 'lightness' was not to be achieved here. Nevertheless, the effective stage-worthiness of the earlier work, which surprised the poet by its 'high seriousness', must have been a reminder that the subjects to which Strauss responded best were those which described the day-to-day human condition – 'themes' which balanced the serious against the comic, a mixture of love, tears, laughter, intrigue and above all reconciliation. It can be no accident that these qualities so characteristic of *Rosenkavalier*, *Ariadne* and *Intermezzo* were revived to such splendid effect. It was, indeed, a work in this *genre* for which Strauss had angled at the outset of the *Helena* negotiations – 'something delicate, amusing and warmhearted'[17] – and which Hofmannsthal, despite initial good intentions, had found himself unable to deliver. But in a letter he held out a distinct, if distant promise with the first intimation of the existence of a *Fiaker* comedy – the seed from which *Arabella* was eventually to spring.

When I allow my thoughts to rove beyond *Helena* and try to absorb your wish that we might succeed once again in producing something like *Rosenkavalier* (but not a copy of it!), then *Intermezzo* (which I look forward to hearing at Dresden in December) provides the most exact cue for the line along which my imagination will have to travel, and is certain to give me definite stimulus and inspiration. The work I took in hand a few days ago will perhaps show you, on the other hand, better than anything else, what I can do in my present state – fourteen years after *Rosenkavalier* – in the field towards which you wish to draw me. For last week I completed a tragedy in prose[18] on which I have been at work since 1920 and, in order to relax from the strain, I have picked out one of the most light-hearted and attractive of my subjects, a Viennese comedy which I mean to put on the stage in the costume of the 1880's.[19]

Arabella had the potential to become the masterpiece of their collaboration. A great fund of technical experience was now at Strauss's and Hofmannsthal's disposal derived from a chain of experiments running from *Rosenkavalier* to *Intermezzo*. All those elements, which brought the 'dialogue' opera to the peak of its development, could be brought to bear on the specific needs of the newly proposed work. In literary terms the text offered scope for that domestic 'ceremonial', in the lovers' encounters and in the 'sacrament' of betrothal, so dear to Hofmannsthal's heart. Neither is the melodic warmth of *Rosenkavalier* lacking, and if the lyric flow is not as vivid as heretofore, it takes on an aristocratic restraint born of

2   Hugo von Hofmannsthal in 1929, the year of his death

high craftsmanship and skill. The lyric qualities of the text represent Hofmannsthal at his best, with a congenial uncomplicated tale, cast in a loosely 'poetic' style whose rhythmic flexibility is well suited to the operetta manner which he himself envisaged and for which the composer had pressed.

So for the first time since the epic uncertainties of *Die Frau ohne Schatten* and *Die ägyptische Helena*, the collaboration at last approached home ground. If the second and third acts of *Arabella* do not fully realise the dramatic perfection of the first, the fate which removed Hofmannsthal before the dream had reached fulfilment is to blame. The composer, paying poignant tribute to 'this genius, this great poet, this sensitive collaborator, this kind friend, this unique talent!', hails 'the wonderful libretto which he [Hofmannsthal] sent me so shortly before his tragic end', which will remain 'a last glorious page in the work of this noble, pure, high-minded man'.[20] *Arabella* has survived, through the equivalent merit of music and text.

3 Costume sketch: *Fortune-teller* (Gustav Oláh); Budapest
Arabella premiere, 1935 – a markedly gipsy-like concept

4   Costume sketch: *Mandryka and his servants* (Gustav Oláh), Budapest *Arabella* premiere, 1935. Authentically Hungarian in design

5 Costume sketch: *Arabella and Zdenka* (Gustav Oláh); Budapest *Arabella*, 1935. Act 1 *finale*

6   Costume sketch: *Fiakermilli* (Gustav Oláh); Budapest *Arabella* premiere, 1935. Distinctly nationalistic in flavour, this design shows the influence of Strauss's other celebrated coloratura part, Zerbinetta in *Ariadne*.

2 *Synopsis*

The action of *Arabella* takes place in the Vienna of the 1860s, the first act being set in the private salon of a fashionable hotel overlooking the Kärntnerstraße, where Count Waldner, his wife, Adelaide, and their two daughters are staying. Waldner, a retired cavalry officer and inveterate gambler, having squandered his means at cards, is on the verge of bankruptcy. The only recourse is for his elder daughter, Arabella, a girl of outstanding beauty and charm, to contract a brilliant marriage. For this reason alone has the ruinous expenditure of a prolonged stay in the capital been incurred. To avoid the expense of 'bringing out' two girls in one season, it has been decided that the younger, Zdenka, should masquerade as a youth – which has the additional advantage of narrowing the competitive field in the marriage stakes.

The stratagem, plausible on account of Zdenka's short hair and slim figure, is fraught with complications, for she has fallen in love with Matteo, one of Arabella's discarded suitors. He, believing her to be the son of the house, makes her his confidant, pleading with her to intercede with her sister on his behalf. To Zdenka's chagrin, Matteo, in Adelaide's view not rich enough, has been forbidden the Waldners' apartments. Living only for his visits and afraid of losing him, she encourages him, despite Arabella's coldness, with false hopes, and fuels his ardour with love letters purporting to be in Arabella's hand. Time, however is running out: the last of Adelaide's jewellery has been pawned, and soon, to Zdenka's despair, they will be forced to leave the city. Arabella, meanwhile, currently pursued by three lovers – a trio of counts the most eligible of whom is Elemer – is in a dilemma. The man of her dreams, 'Der Richtige' (the right man), has not materialised. Today is Ash Wednesday; the last ball of the season, the cabbies', or 'Fiakerball', takes place this very evening; she can delay no longer.

17

Act 1

As the curtain rises, Adelaide, seeking reassurance over the worsening family situation, is deep in consultation with a Fortune-teller; the disguised Zdenka, intermittently staving off creditors, busies herself with household accounts at a side table. The Fortune-teller, her dexterity with the cards brilliantly depicted by the orchestral strings, at first offers Adelaide little comfort, predicting more ill luck for her gambler husband. Pressed about the hoped-for engagement, the gipsy dismisses Matteo's prospects – to Adelaide's relief and Zdenka's bitter disappointment – raising maternal hopes by her vision of a wealthy stranger ('right man' horn *Motiv*), summoned by letter, from a distant land of forests as bridegroom. Adelaide, believing this new suitor to be Elemer, is overjoyed, but elation is cut short by hints of trouble: Arabella's hesitations, a quarrel, and a duel, are prophesied, as well as the appearance of an unidentified girl who will endanger the successful outcome. These revelations force Adelaide to admit Zdenka's identity; embarrassed, she ushers the sibyl into the next room, to continue the discussion in private.

Alone, Zdenka gives free rein to her emotions. The creditors' demands have confirmed her conviction that the days in Vienna are numbered. Soon she will be separated from Matteo for ever. An anguished orchestral statement in E major (love key) combines three important musical ideas (Ex. 2.1) associated respectively with Matteo (a), Zdenka's feminity (b) and 'passion' (c), a *Motiv* which dogs the emotional fortunes of both characters throughout the course of the opera.

Ex. 2.1

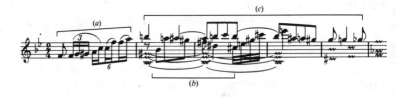

Confused and anxious, she eavesdrops at the door of her mother's room as the clarinet (Ex. 2.2), 'fluttering' nervously above a furtive bass tremolo, presents the characteristic Zdenka *Motiv*:

Ex. 2.2

Her mother's determination to ban Matteo from the Waldner apartments produces a passionate outburst. Beside herself, she prays for a miracle – her father's success at cards, or the death of a rich aunt – 'If only Arabella would fall in love with Matteo', she vows, 'I would sacrifice all my hopes, all my feelings, and wear breeches for the rest of my life.'

Matteo's entry is marked Ex. 2.3, both by *Motiv* and key (E minor), in the orchestral strings.

Ex. 2.3

Despite the warmth of Arabella's letters (written of course by Zdenka), Matteo is puzzled by her continued coldness toward him. Jealously he plies Zdenka with questions; she, with a pretty melodic phrase, 'That's how a girl is. . .', attributes Arabella's seemingly irrational behaviour to bashfulness, attempting to allay his doubts with the promise of yet another love letter. Such a token, he says, is his last hope, and Zdenka is his only friend. If she fails him he has no recourse other than military exile or his revolver. Matteo's departure leaves Zdenka desolate – the music rises once more to a passionate climax. Drawing upon the depth of her own feelings, she can summon up words enough to furnish him with hundreds of love letters but the phrases needed to convince Arabella that he is the only suitor worthy of her hand are more difficult to find – ironically, it is on the latter that her own destiny depends.

So far, the action has been furthered by a succession of dialogue scenes with swift, purposeful, *parlando* style and restrained scoring, briefly interrupted by the two passionate Zdenka interludes. Now, Zdenka's agitated D minor mood of protestation dissolves into a warm, generous F major, with the arrival of Arabella. The glowing shapeliness of the important oboe melody which accompanies her entrance (Ex. 2.4) establishes her grace and charm. A sudden harmonic 'stillness', the gold-hued delicacy of instrumental texture and the expressive poise of the vocal line leave one in no doubt that the heroine has arrived.

Ex. 2.4

Fresh from her morning walk, Arabella graciously dismisses her attendant. She is haunted by the memory of the strange, attractive man who has of late lingered on her doorstep. With excited enquiry she admires a bouquet of roses – petulantly rejecting them when they are identified as a gift from Matteo. Zdenka, shocked by such wilful behaviour, upbraids her sister for encouraging the attentions of her three noble suitors (the Counts), putting in so eloquent a plea for Matteo that Arabella is alerted to the true state of her sister's heart. This half-unconscious confession of love for Matteo strengthens Arabella's determination to put an end to this boyish masquerade. 'I'd rather stay a boy for ever, than turn into a cold, proud coquette like you!' remarks Zdenka snappishly. Arabella realises the futility of argument. 'Matteo is simply not the right man for me', she explains, rationalising her feelings in a lyrical outpouring based on a seminal idea (Ex. 2.5) close to that which introduces Mandryka later in the act ('Er ist der Richtige nicht für mich').

Ex. 2.5

A climax is now reached in the Arabella/Zdenka duet ('Aber der Richtige'), again in F major. Here, against a luminous background of divided strings, the voices, exquisitely blended, proclaim a unity which symbolises the sisters' love for one another. The Slavonic folksong melody so transformed is an apt source for the 'Der Richtige' *Motiv*.

> *Arabella*: But the right man for me, if he is to be found in all this
> world,
> will suddenly appear and stand before me
> and he will look at me, and I at him,
> and there will be no doubts and no questionings,
> and I will be so happy and as obedient as a child.

> *Zdenka*: I don't understand, but I love you too much to be able
> to judge
> your actions – I only want you to be happy
> with someone who is worthy of your love
> and to help you to realise that happiness.[1]

The reverie is interrupted by sleigh bells in the street, a reminder that Arabella has promised to spend the afternoon with Count Elemer. Skittish once more, she pokes fun at the amorous trio courting her. Neither Dominik nor Lamoral, not even Elemer, has touched her heart – nevertheless time is not on her side; failing all else, she will have to accept Elemer before the evening is out. As Zdenka envisages the effect upon Matteo, Arabella moves to the window. Suddenly serious, she tells of the mysterious, attractive stranger who had lingered near the hotel that morning. He had regarded her so fixedly that she had been certain it was for her that he was waiting; she could have sworn that he would send her flowers; what joy the gift would have brought her. Seizing her cue, Zdenka snatches up Matteo's discarded roses, one last plea on his behalf, a gesture cut short by Elemer's entrance, 'This is the day I have been waiting for' ('Heut ist mein Tag!').

Striding in to wild *Polacca* rhythms and a fanfare-like horn *Motiv*, Elemer assumes command, proclaiming his day's lordship over Arabella, which includes squiring her for the afternoon, as well as later at the ball. Between them, the three Counts have determined her fate; Arabella, put out by such treatment, warns Elemer not to be too confident. She is still unsure of her feelings – this very night, something wonderful might happen to make her dreams come true. Elemer brushes her doubts aside, as an important rising *Motiv* (Ex. 2.6) associated with his impetuous nature, heralds an exhilarating hymn to the charms of this peerless woman who will soon be his.

Ex. 2.6

Das   an - dre   wird Kom - men

Rushing out to exercise the horses, he is barely able to stifle his annoyance when Arabella demands Zdenka's presence as chaperone for their afternoon drive in the Prater.

From the window, Arabella admires Elemer's horses outside the hotel. Without warning, the music plunges into Ab major; the abrupt change of key, and the suppressed excitement of pianissimo, tremolo strings, reflecting her sudden agitation. There opposite the hotel, stands her mysterious stranger. Breathlessly, and to instrumental evocations of the 'right man' *Motiv*, she beckons her sister over to admire those 'great serious eyes', which seem to seek her window. As the stranger retires, so Arabella turns disappointedly away. The sisters withdraw to prepare themselves for their drive.

Adelaide returns, accompanied by her husband fresh from unsuccessful gambling. Tired and depressed, he rifles aimlessly through the post. There is still no reply from his old regimental comrade, Mandryka, a rich Croatian nobleman, to whom he had optimistically sent a portrait of Arabella. His hopes of a match seem destined to failure. In spite of Adelaide's protests, 'God in heaven! My pretty child wed to an old man!', he insists that the first opportunity of a rich marriage must be taken. There has been too much shilly-shallying already. Still pinning her hopes on the Fortune-teller, the Countess lists possible alternatives, but Waldner is sceptical. Since even the emerald brooch has gone, there is nothing left to pawn. As a final blow to his pride the hotel staff have been ordered to withdraw his credit. Adelaide retires, leaving him to his musings.

Despite his strict instructions to the contrary, the waiter announces a caller. Fearful of creditors, Waldner is inclined to refuse the visiting card, but, catching sight of Mandryka's name, rises to embrace his old comrade. He is taken aback by the stranger who confronts him. The formal introductions are 'pointed' by the noble Eb major Mandryka theme (Ex. 2.7), as the visitor blames the tattered and bloodied state of Waldner's letter, proffered in lieu of credentials, on a recent hunting encounter with a bear in his native Croatian forests.

Ex. 2.7

His uncle, Waldner's old friend, has recently died; 'I am the only
Mandryka now'. The astounded Count tactfully confirms that
Arabella, whose portrait has captivated Mandryka, is still unwed.
Mandryka probes, with great nobility of expression, Waldner's reasons for the approach to his deceased uncle. What if the old man had
fancied the girl, he demands, and had hurried to Vienna to claim her
for his bride? At last Mandryka comes to the point, tendering, in a
triumphant aria, his own proposal for Arabella's hand ('Mein sind
die Wälder'):

> Mine are the forests, mine are the villages.
> Four thousand serfs pray for the success of my suit,
> and I plead with outstretched hands, I ask you sir;
> give your lady daughter into my care
> give to me, as my wife,
> the girl who for the last fourteen weeks,
> has reigned as mistress of my heart.[2]

There follows a 'furiant'-like ballade during which, whilst relating
the incident with the bear, and an impatiently borne convalescence
which delayed him, he reveals his enormous wealth. A purse stuffed
full of bank notes, 'That was a forest. . .now it's just a few scraps of
paper', has a remarkable effect on Waldner, who can hardly believe
his eyes. Mandryka courteously insists, 'Do please, help yourself':
'Teschek, bedien' Dich!' The overjoyed Count, extracts, with a show
of reluctance, two one-thousand gulden notes and offers to seal the
bargain by introducing his daughter at once. Mandryka restrains
him. The moment of encounter has a 'holiness' about it – it is almost
a sacrament: both parties must be sufficiently prepared ('Das ist ein
Fall von andrer Art'). He will await Arabella's commands, perhaps
they can meet later, or at the evening's ball. . .When Mandryka has
left Waldner has to pinch himself to make sure that he is awake.
'Hab' ich geträumt?' ('Did I dream it all?'), he asks himself; the reality of the banknotes reassures him. Half crazed with joy, and to the
astonishment of Zdenka who has now re-entered, he seizes hat and

stick and dashes off to the casino, to delirious cries of 'Teschek, bedien' Dich'.

All this is beyond Zdenka's comprehension – for her, tragedy is closing in. Tonight she will see Matteo for the last time; tomorrow the family will have to leave. Matteo puts his head round the door. He has evaded Waldner in the passage-way and wants to see Arabella. Once more he demands the 'promised' letter, which Zdenka pledges to hand over that evening at the ball. Challenging her to keep her word, he slips away.

Now, dressed for her excursion, Arabella returns, and sends Zdenka off to get changed. Zdenka's taunting 'Your Elemer!' rings oddly in her ears. 'My Elemer! How strange that sounds', she muses, as she weighs up the pros and cons of the situation. Does she really want Elemer? What are her true feelings in respect to him? Matteo is definitely a non-starter – a mere boy, but what about the mysterious stranger? – if only she could see him just once more! Bemoaning the lot of woman, who cannot choose, but must wait to be chosen, she gradually puts her unhappiness aside. Her stranger will certainly be a contentedly married man and that's an end to it! Dismissing her doubts, she looks forward to the excitement of the coming ball. Gradually the rhythm of the waltz pervades the score, very properly closing the act on a note of optimism, as Arabella sweeps Zdenka through the door and out into the street. The curtain falls.

> My Elemer! How strange it sounds. . .
> He mine – I his. Why does that disturb me so?
> Overwhelming me with feelings that I can't understand
> and such unaccountable longings. . .
> Longings for Matteo perhaps?
> Because he says he can't live without me
> and looks at me with such child-like eyes?
> No, these sighs are not for Matteo!
> If only I could see my stranger once again!
> If only I could hear his voice, just once
> Then – then perhaps he'd turn out to be like all the others –
> What did Zdenka say? That we women have to wait until we're
>   chosen
> if we're not chosen, then we're lost, –
> But marriage with Elemer, . . .
> Why does the thought of it agitate me so?
> It's as if I was walking over someone's grave?
> Is it that stranger to whom I've never even spoken,
> whose spirit reaches out to me, in the darkness?
> My God – He'll certainly be a married man
> and then I shall never see him, nor even want to again!. . .

But today! Today is Ash Wednesday
And this evening it's my ball –
of which I am to be the queen. . .[3]

Act 2

Act 2 is set in the pillared vestibule of a public ballroom in the Leopoldstadt district. The cabbies' ball is in full swing. Arabella, followed by admirers, is ushered by her mother down the great central stairway, towards Waldner and Mandryka, who wait below in evening dress. This whole concept – Arabella's descent, her first encounter with Mandryka, and the music which accompanies it (Ex. 2.8, derived from Ex. 2.5 and Ex. 2.7) – has considerable structural importance in the opera. The passage is later paralleled and transformed in the Act 3 *finale*, where the 'prize' at the foot of the staircase is manifest at last in the forgiveness, reconciliation and commitment of the lovers' embrace.

Ex. 2.8

Mandryka, waiting to be introduced, gazes on Arabella for the first time. He is spellbound by her beauty. 'She is like an angel stepped down from heaven itself', he whispers to Waldner. Arabella, too, is overcome at the sight of Mandryka, whom she immediately recognises as the stranger who has haunted her dreams. Taken momentarily aback, she turns aside to collect herself, but the impatient Waldner precipitates the introductions and leaves.

The couple strike up a somewhat embarrassed conversation, interrupted by the three Counts in turn, to waltz strains from the adjoining salon, attempting to spirit Arabella away. Naïvely, Mandryka delivers a moving eulogy on his former wife ('Ich habe eine Frau gehabt'):

> I had a wife once – so beautiful, so good and so pure
> I was only granted a mere two years of happiness with her
> before the Lord God suddenly called her to him –
> I was too young, and quite unworthy of such an angel.[4]

Excusing his sentimentality, 'Please forgive me! I'm a clumsy peasant', and ignoring her curiosity about his acquisition of her portrait in 'far Slavonia', he plunges into a passionate description of the impact her beauty has made upon him. Setting out in the key of F major, this passage flirts momentarily with the E major (love key) goal, before reaching a powerful emotional climax in F♯ major ('Sie sind schön, Arabella'):

> You are so beautiful – there is a power in your features,
> which impresses itself upon the soft wax of my soul!
> Such a power is very great over a simple man,
> A man of the woods and fields such as I,
> He will become obsessed by dreams
> He will be as one possessed, enchanted,
> And the needs of his soul will dictate a decision
> Which once made will brook no denial
> Which will demand immediate action.[5]

Refusing to be won under false pretences, Arabella goes to some lengths to explain the delicate family situation. Mandryka brushes aside her doubts, beseeching her to accept his hand, to be the mistress of his heart and to reign over his dominions ('Ihren Stammbaum, Arabella, den tragen Sie in Ihrem Gesicht geschrieben!').

Moved, Arabella recalls the words of her Act 1 duet with Zdenka, the melodic 'kernel' of which, the *'Der Richtige' Motiv*, combining with Ex. 2.7 now permeates the orchestral texture, the voice rising to a melismatic climax. As she recognises in Mandryka the fulfilment of her hopes, he relates a traditional betrothal custom which, in his own country, would seal their union. The moment is near; motivic figures and phrases first dimly perceived, gradually crystallise into coherent form as the music flows towards the tonal inevitability of E major, and the opening strains of the love duet ('Du wirst mein Gebieter sein'):

> *Mandryka*: Thus, the bright still Danube, flowing past my house,
> has brought you to me, you most beautiful of women!
> And this very evening, if you were a girl from one of
> my villages,
> you'd have to go, at dusk, to the spring behind your
> father's house,
> and fill a goblet brim-full of clear water,
> and bring it to me as I stand before the threshold,
> to affirm
> before God and men, that I am your betrothed,
> most lovely child!

Arabella:	I have never known anyone else like you
	You bring with you a quality of life which is all your own,
	and that which runs counter to it
	simply doesn't exist or matter, as far as you're concerned.
Mandryka:	I can only continue thus, if I have something to live up to
	So now, high above me as you are, I choose you for my wife,
	and where I am master, so shall you be mistress
	and where I am lord, there shall you command.
Arabella:	You shall be my lord and I will serve you
	Your house shall be my house, in one grave shall we be buried –
	I belong to you now, for always and for ever.[6]

The couple stand transfixed, as a radiant orchestral postlude (unison inversion of Ex. 2.5 on first and second violins, counterpointed with trombone echoes of the duet melody), gradually restores a more normal emotional temperature. Arabella decides that she must dance farewell to her girlhood. She proposes that Mandryka return to his hotel, but he pleads that as her betrothed, his place is at her side. She is to ignore his presence, to enjoy herself and to do just as she pleases.

A waltz signals the entry from the ballroom of a throng of dancers led by Count Dominik, among them the traditional cabbies' mascot, 'Fiakermilli', who welcomes Arabella and proclaims her queen of the evening's festivities. The Polka rhythms and extravagant coloratura with which her song is laced reflect her pert, flirtatious vivacity ('Die Wiener Herr'n verstehn sich auf die Astronomie'):

> Expert in astronomy
> These Viennese gentlemen! You see –
> Each in his way's a connoisseur
> Without knowing why, with no degree,
> And quick to pick out some new star –
> And hail it mistress of their sphere!
> (These Viennese, that's how they are!)
> Thus we proclaim at their decree –
> That you queen of the *Fiakerball* shall be![7]

The orchestra strikes up another waltz and Milli distributes flowers before leading Dominik back to the ballroom followed by the rest of the company.

While Adelaide and Mandryka exchange civilities, Zdenka, keeping well out of sight, attempts to pacify Matteo, who is jealously watching Arabella's every move, and repeats his threat of self-exile. Waldner joins his wife and son-in-law-to-be, as Mandryka spares no expense in ordering champagne and wagon-loads of flowers. Until the meal which Mandryka has ordered, the party retires to the ballroom.

A more serious mood ensues as Arabella enters on Dominik's arm. Genuinely moved, she bids farewell to the earliest of her lovers in this, the first of three cameo sketches which provide a lyric centrepiece to the act. The character of each of these contrasted miniatures owes much to Strauss's orchestration, the graceful wind-band sonorities of Dominik's dismissal giving way to the passionately scored Elemer episode, in which his demands are rebuffed with sensitivity. Lamoral emerges as the most endearing of her three admirers, his gentle expansiveness owing much to the homophonic movement of strings and woodwind. A brief interruption – a single chaste goodbye kiss, chromatically 'pointed' in the orchestra, grants him a single moment of ecstasy before they are swallowed up in the throng of dancers.

The swirling couples are briefly glimpsed through the open door of the ballroom; in the vestibule, waiters deck the supper tables. A grim-faced Matteo is accosted by Zdenka, who categorically reassures him of Arabella's passion. As she hands over Arabella's supposed letter, Mandryka, casting an eye over the supper arrangements, saunters out of the ballroom. His attention is caught by Matteo's exclamation, as he discovers, in the envelope Zdenka has given him, the key to Arabella's sleeping apartment. Mandryka's casual interest turns to outrage as he learns that his betrothed will receive Matteo, this very evening, in her room. 'As surely as that key unlocks her door', promises Zdenka ambiguously, 'so surely will she who gives it to you, do everything in her power this evening, to bring you happiness.' She exits, followed by Matteo, who, to Mandryka's fury, openly gloats over his good fortune.

Mandryka's reaction is violent – he orders Welko and Djura to apprehend 'the man with the key', but it is too late. He is half inclined to pass over the incident – after all, Arabella is still, as far as he knows, enjoying herself in the ballroom. Nevertheless, a spark has been ignited which, smouldering through a brief dalliance between Adelaide and Dominik, is fanned into a jealous blaze by reports that

Arabella is nowhere to be found. Fiakermilli's request that he 'Give the ball back its queen' drives him into a towering rage as the company assembles. Champagne flows freely at Mandryka's expense and he leads the revelry, indulging in an outrageous flirtation with Milli. Further search by Welko reveals a note, from Arabella, 'I'm going home now, goodnight. From tomorrow I shall be yours.' Mandryka's worst fears seem to be realised. He plies the company with drink; torn between fury and self-pity, he breaks into a wild satirical ballad (a musical travesty of the E major love duet), clasping Milli, who supplies a flamboyant yodelling chorus to his song:

> Walking through a forest: don't know which one
> Came across a girl there: somebody's daughter
> Stepped hard on her foot: don't know which one
> Then she started crying: can't think why though
> Just look at the wretch: that's what he thinks love is.
>
> Good thing to give him wine in a barrel
> Give him wine with no glass to drink from
> Make him drink from the heavy barrel
> Make him suffer till he gains his senses
>
> Good thing to give myself to him
> Give myself but not give him my bed
> Make the fool sleep on bare earth
> Make him suffer till he gains some sense
>
> Today she's gone home to her paramour
> After tonight, she belongs to me
> Give us a kiss – Milli!
> What does a countess's room cost here in Vienna?[8]

At the height of this scene, Adelaide, outraged by Mandryka's behaviour and his insinuations, summons her husband to defend the honour of his wife and daughter. Waldner also receives somewhat cavalier treatment but takes a more hard-headed view of things. Expressing surprise at Arabella's disappearance, he proposes to run her to earth at the hotel – where this 'little misunderstanding' will be cleared up. Perhaps Mandryka would like to come too; 'It would be a very great honour indeed', comes the sarcastic reply. Mustering his card-playing cronies, Waldner shepherds the party to the door. Mandryka pauses to address the company, inviting them to be his guests for the remainder of the evening. As the curtain falls, the revellers lift their glasses in a noisy toast, above which soar Milli's exultant trillings.

Act 3

The brilliantly scored orchestral introduction to this act (predictably in E major) depicts the passage of love between Zdenka and Matteo. Two musical *Motive* are significant here, the first (Ex. 2.1b) defining Zdenka's femininity, and the second (Ex. 2.1c), a tense, emotional idea, representing their shared passion. The 'flutterings' of Zdenka's Ex. 2.2 and Matteo's urgent personality *Motiv* (Ex. 2.3) have important psychological roles to play, as do two significant 'Arabella' figures, which, as they weave their way through the score, keep in mind Matteo's delusions. As passion subsides, and the climax dissolves it is Zdenka's Ex. 2.2 that 'takes the floor', a distillation of the ecstatic Ex. 2.1c, which, echoing ballroom memories, glides reflectively into a languorous waltz.

The prolonged upbeat of the waltz heralds the rise of the curtain. The scene is set in the Waldners' hotel vestibule. Matteo, in shirt-sleeves, emerges furtively from Zdenka's bedroom on to the first floor landing, approached from the hotel reception area by an imposing stairway. Startled by the doorbell, announcing Arabella's return, the mildly embarrassed Matteo leaves. Arabella is pensive. As she ponders the events of an evening which has transformed her world, the lilting G major charm of the waltz reflects her happiness. She sings of Mandryka, their new-found love, and future life together ('Über seine Felder'):

> Together we shall drive across his fields
> and through his tall, silent forests –
> whose strength and stillness is so much part of him;
> and his men will ride out to meet us.
> 'This is your mistress', he'll say,
> 'whom I have brought', he'll tell them,
> 'from Vienna, from the *Kaiserstadt*,
> to which, however, she'll never want to return –
> all she wants now is to be with me in my forests.'[9]

This gentle *Lied* recalls elements of the Act 2 love duet (flutes and oboes), weaving together a distinctive group of Arabella/Mandryka themes (including Exx. 2.5 and 2.7) in a passage of polyphonic refinement and restraint. Dramatically, this pause for reflection constitutes an important stage in Arabella's progress towards emotional maturity. Her vision has now taken tangible form. She recognises Mandryka as her destiny, and comes to terms, for the first time, with the reality of love. This, in Hofmannsthal's terms, is a development of the 'self-encounter' of the Act 1 *finale*. The unshakeable certainty of this love gives her new confidence and inner certainty. During the act, she sits in the eye of an emotional storm which, raging about her, can hurt but not destroy. The truth ('Wahrheit') which she has won, and which she represents, is love, and proof against calumny. It is from the steadfast inner conviction expounded in this short scene that her powers of healing, reconciliation and forgiveness stem – it is crucial to the psychological development of the act.

Arabella's *reverie* is interrupted by Matteo, who reappears on the balcony above. He is taken aback at the sight of the girl who, he believes, was only minutes ago in his arms, now up, dressed, and apparently ready to go out. Arabella is equally astonished at his presence: 'why are you here so late?' she enquires. His demeanour is puzzling, and his knowing air and uncharacteristic gallantry are not to her taste. She is, moreover, irritated by his refusal to believe that she has just come home. Matteo is vexed by what he interprets as an affectation of prudishness on her part. He interprets her attitude as some sort of joke, an 'unfathomable girlish secret', beyond man's comprehension. Thwarting her attempts to go upstairs, he tries to slip under the guard of her reserve; overcome by his feelings, he pours out his thanks for favours received in a few brief, passionately intense phrases. 'Your thanks! Whatever for?' asks the astonished Arabella, bringing him back to earth. Exasperated, he compliments her on her virtuosity as a 'quick-change' artist. She orders him to stand aside; if he doesn't move, she will call for help. Throughout this altercation the music, reflecting Matteo's mounting passion, progresses towards a powerfully emotive E major climax. Driven almost to the point of madness, Matteo begs for one final tender glance before he honours his 'bedroom promise' and relinquishes his claim on her for ever. Before Arabella has the chance to demand an explanation, Waldner, Adelaide and Mandryka arrive, intent on solving the mystery of her premature departure from the ball.

The discovery of Arabella *tête à tête* with Matteo, whom he immediately recognises as the recipient of the key to Arabella's room, confirms Mandryka in his suspicions. Responding with barbed politeness to her surprised but friendly greeting, he begs leave to withdraw. Welko is to pack at once; 'We take the first available train home', he declares, cutting short her explanations. Adelaide, horrified, rounds angrily on Matteo, but Waldner, enjoining the sceptical Mandryka to patience, draws Arabella aside to quiz her about her conduct. 'My child! tell me, did this officer escort you home from the ball?' he asks, warmer string tones nourishing the 'cool' precision of the orchestral wind as she quietly reassures him on the propriety of her conduct. Relieved and anxious to return to his cards, he is prepared to dismiss the whole incident, but Mandryka is not so easily satisfied. He impugns Arabella more directly, but she proclaims her innocence, gently upbraiding him for his unwarranted suspicions as her voice rises above the forgiveness *Motiv* (Ex. 2.9) in the strings ('Mandryka, hören Sie'):

Ex. 2.9

> Mandryka, listen to me,
> As truly as there's a God in Heaven
> you have nothing to forgive me for!
> It is my place, rather, to try and forgive you
> for the things that you have said
> and for the tone in which you have said them.[10]

Stung by her reply he rounds on her so harshly that Matteo steps forward to assert his prerogative of defending Arabella's honour in mortal combat. She is appalled by his temerity; the only man to possess such rights is Mandryka, her betrothed: 'What on earth have you to do with the matter of my honour?' Matteo is embarrassed; he doesn't want to compromise Arabella further, but when she presses him to deny the 'supposed' relationship between them, his hesitations are interpreted as proof of her guilt. Mandryka's accusations now become more explicit, their enormity even stimulating the bewildered Waldner to send for his (long-since pawned) pistols, whilst Arabella, dignified but heart-broken, resigns herself to her fate – 'Let what must come, come; life is nothing to me if this man is so weak that he cannot believe me but deserts me without any reason at all.'

Matteo, moved by Arabella's distress, decides to renounce his, as he believes, just claim on her affections, to clear her name. 'You must all have misunderstood me', he protests, 'It is all my fault! If anyone should be punished, it is I.' His 'confession' convinces no one, least of all Mandryka, who sorrowfully urges Arabella not to perjure herself further but to admit the unfaithfulness which has shamed him so. 'By all that I hold sacred and holy, Mandryka', she insists, 'I have told you the truth' ('Bei meiner Seele und Seligkeit, Mandryka, die Wahrheit ist bei mir!'). Bitterly, he recapitulates the events of the evening. Did he not see a certain youth give Arabella's key to Matteo? Arabella realises that the youth must be Zdenka; she must in some way be involved in this *débâcle*. Unwilling to expose her sister, she refuses further comment and the tight-lipped, furious Mandryka sends for weapons. He and Matteo will settle the affair between them, alone, in the Winter-garden.

This scene, set in Strauss's dialogue or conversational manner, has no 'set pieces'. Arabella's music alone employs any real degree of lyrical consistency; so the composer clearly set out to distinguish her from the other characters. Amid the confusion and deceit, the nobility and high-mindedness of Arabella's character, which through the intimate, confidential quality of her opening *Lied* has already enlisted the sympathy of the audience, is confirmed and finally established. Strauss's employment of spoken dialogue at the end of the scene, as Mandryka prepares for the duel, greatly enhances the climactic effect.

The suspense is broken by an anguished cry of 'Papa! Mama!' from above, which rivets everyone's attention on the first floor landing: it is Zdenka, still clad in her negligée, her hair loose and dishevelled, who rushes down the stairs to throw herself at her father's feet. The waves of the Danube, inextricably interwoven with the nervous flutterings of the Zdenka *Motiv* (Ex. 2), well up in the orchestral strings as she proclaims her intention to drown herself before dawn – 'Then you will all forgive me, even Papa!' The compassionate Arabella, setting her own misery aside, throws a protective arm about her shoulders, as Waldner, sensing that her story holds the key to the evening's events, bids her make a clean breast of everything.

It is to Arabella alone that Zdenka will confide. The orchestral lyricism grows, as she shyly admits her deception of Matteo, who responds to the sound of his name uttered in such tones. 'What sweet voice is it that calls me?' he sings; 'It is the voice of one who has deceived you, Matteo', Zdenka replies. She will not be comforted, although Matteo is now completely captivated by her. She asks forgiveness of both these people whom she has wronged, hiding her face in shame at her unmaidenly behaviour. The music has now veered towards Strauss's emotional 'flat' keys (see p. 78), as Arabella proffers advice which holds meaning for Mandryka: 'If love that is too great for containment needs any excuse or justification, then you must indeed ask his forgiveness!' Matteo makes it plain that in his eyes Zdenka can do no wrong.

The truth of the situation now begins to dawn upon the company. Mandryka is aghast at his mistake, and has given up hope of Arabella's forgiveness. The arrival of Welko and Djura with weapons provides the cue for Waldner to renew his challenge; but Mandryka's immediate concern is the repair of his relationship with Arabella, who is too concerned about Zdenka to pay heed to him. Now, with immense tact and with a significance that this time does not escape her lover, she transforms Zdenka's peccadillo into an example of unmatched love, steadfastness and commitment. She herself, she assures her tearful sister, has learned an important lesson from her action ('Zdenkerl, du bist die Bess're von uns zweien'):

A   Little Zdenka, you are the better of the two of us
    you have a more loving heart, and nothing exists for you,
    nothing at all save that which your heart dictates.
    Thank you so much for the lesson you have taught me:
    that we shouldn't be always wanting and demanding –
    weighing the cost, haggling and being miserly,
    but we should give and love always and without measure.

Z   You speak so gently to me! You show no anger!
    Your goodness is beyond words to describe.
    I know you better than I know anyone else,
    and all that I do, I do out of love for you.
    I wanted to slip quietly away
    without disturbing anyone! But you understand me
    and won't forsake me whatever happens now![11]

'Whatever happens now!' ('Was jetzt noch kommt!') – this phrase, echoed in turn by Mandryka (as yet uncertain of Arabella's forgiveness), Waldner, whose thoughts are still on the possibility of a duel, and Arabella herself, gains, by repetition, musical emphasis and meaning. For Mandryka a future without Arabella seems bleak – he turns dispiritedly away – but her unexpected, quiet 'Mandryka' halts him. A broad, expansive descending phrase depicts his wonderment as he recognises a potential forgiveness of which he feels himself unworthy. She softly stills his fears: 'We weren't to blame! We'll need all our reserves of good will to cope with whatever happens next!' 'Was jetzt noch kommt?. . .' asks Mandryka; 'What's going to happen now?. . . We're going to celebrate an engagement', he declares triumphantly. Grasping Matteo by the hand, he leads him across to Waldner, on his behalf to plead for the bestowal of Zdenka's hand, and the parental blessing ('Brautwerbung kommt!'):

> With this gentleman, most noble sir,
> I appear before you, I make obeisance and ask
> on his behalf, as his friend,
> that you will not refuse to bestow upon him
> the hand of this young woman.
> That you will not deny to him the boon
> which great love has conferred upon him.[12]

'Matteo! Papa! What does it mean?' asks Zdenka, as the first horn counterpoints her anxiety with a variant of Ex. 2.2, 'Don't I have to go away after all?' 'You must now be happy, just as you deserve to be', sings Arabella in exultantly noble tones. Deeply moved, Waldner kisses his younger daughter, shakes Matteo by the hand and embraces his tearful wife. Relieved of further embarrassment, he musters his retinue of card-playing cronies in the conservatory, where the important business of the evening is to be concluded. The onlookers, the hotel guests who had gathered to watch the proceedings, retire to their beds as Adelaide conducts the tired but happy Zdenka to her room and Arabella gently sends Matteo away – tomorrow he may claim Zdenka.

Arabella and Mandryka are at last alone. The music settles on to the E♭ major dominant, prompting, with growing warmth and lyricism, the inevitable but not yet reached reconciliatory outcome. Unconsciously paraphrasing the music which earlier accompanied Mandryka's account of the engagement ritual of his native land, Arabella requests, as she retires for the night, a glass of fresh, cool water from the well in the hotel courtyard. She mounts the staircase, watched longingly by Mandryka until she is out of sight. The hallway darkens as the lamps are extinguished, the gloom mirroring his mood. Welko returns, glass in hand, and his master, with a nod, directs him to Arabella's room. He meditates on his unforgivable stupidity. She left him without a word of tenderness, without a glance; indeed, he reflects, he deserves no better treatment ('Sie gibt mir keinen Blick'):

> She didn't even glance in my direction,
> she just went away, leaving me standing here
> What else do I deserve?
> Who, indeed, deserves anything in this world
> except a fool like me who only merits a thrashing –
> but if only she had looked my way just once –

> even a mere half-glance would have been something!
> All she could think about was a glass of water
> and to be relieved of my presence.
> Perhaps she meant to show her contempt for me –
> if so, at least that's attention of a sort –
> although, God knows, I don't deserve even this much![13]

As he muses, Arabella slips silently on to the landing, the glass of water in her hand. She glances down into the vestibule and her face lights up at the sight of Mandryka standing immobile in the half-light, his back towards her. To music which might have fallen from heaven itself, the celebrated 'staircase' music, slowly and with solemnity, she descends towards him, the consciousness of her symbolic act growing with every step. Suddenly aware of her presence, Mandryka turns, spellbound. At the foot of the stairway, she pauses, addressing him in tones of tenderness and love ('Das war sehr gut, Mandryka'):

> It is good to find you still here, Mandryka,
> It was my pleasure to drink quite alone,
> banishing this nightmare evening from my mind
> and quietly go to bed, our future put aside
> until a bright new day dawned over us.
> But then I sensed your presence in the darkness,
> and moved, heart deep, by some great power on high
> I knew no need of water to refresh me;
> no, for the joyful feelings of my soul
> had yet restored my happiness,
> therefore this brim-full glass I offer to my friend
> to mark the evening that my girlhood ends.[14]

She approaches him, the glass in her outstretched hand as the orchestra again recollects the music of the village betrothal. Mandryka takes it, drains it in one quick draught, before smashing it at his feet.

> As surely as no one else will drink again from this glass,
> So surely do we belong together, you and I, for ever.[15]

Laying her hand on his shoulder, Arabella pledges herself to him for ever. She will remain true, whatever the future holds for them both. 'You will never change, will you?', he implores; 'Indeed, I can't', she answers, sinking into his arms, 'Take me, just as I am.' Suddenly, breaking away, and without a backward glance, she runs swiftly up the stairway to her room. Mandryka watches her tenderly until she is out of sight, as the orchestra's exultant confirmatory strains of the 'right man' theme ring down the final curtain.

3 *The literary sources of the opera*

Arabella had its roots in *Der Rosenkavalier,* as the Strauss/ Hofmannsthal correspondence shows.[1] Musical commentators have, however, generally been inclined to over-emphasise the importance and to misinterpret the nature of the relationship between the two operas. The concept of a 'second *Rosenkavalier*' was in no sense opportunistic, a bid to capitalise upon earlier success, but a legitimate attempt to evoke through association of ideas a creative mood and *rapport* which had already inspired happy results.

The rekindling of Strauss's on-going but so far unrequited 'love affair' with light opera, was now to initiate, 'on the rebound' from the symbolic '*Märchenoper*', *Die Frau ohne Schatten,* a series of more volatile collaborative suggestions which may, with hindsight, be seen to be indicative of the later *Arabella* ethos. This concept of 'lightness' was foreshadowed in the 'nimble-witted', 'operetta-like' *Danaë* sketch which Hofmannsthal submitted to Strauss in 1920,[2] but which, despite Strauss's enthusiasm, 'I feel downright called upon to become the Offenbach of the twentieth century',[3] the poet was unable to complete.[4] Clearly, both collaborators were conscious of a need to re-identify with the congenial and objective comprehensibility of the earlier *Der Rosenkavalier* which had been so successful. Unfortunately, the overt expression of this need, ultimately realised in *Arabella,* has also encouraged misleading and inappropriate comparisons between the two works.

If the promptings for a new opera in a lighter vein apparently came from Strauss, Hofmannsthal was very willing to exploit an idea which would 'Continue exactly the line *Rosenkavalier, Ariadne-Vorspiel, Bürger als Edelmann*', and contribute to the generic uniqueness of each of their works, which he also recognised as characteristic of *Intermezzo*:

Everything I may still do for you must be a thing of its own kind: each one of the earlier works constituted a *genre* of its own. . .I am pleased by the idea that the little opera [*Intermezzo*] which you wrote for yourself in between fits very beautifully into this series of ever-new diversity.[5]

Inevitably, for both men, the idea must have seemed doubly potent after the complexities of *Helena*, which had started life with operetta-like pretensions. For Strauss, an orientation towards *Rosenkavalier* demonstrated less a desire for artistic regression than an attempt to stimulate Hofmannsthal to rediscover the human warmth and easy motivation fundamental to that work. Strauss's practical needs apart, Hofmannsthal's wider vision enabled him, by drawing on ethnic materials from his native Vienna, to make a distinctive contribution along the lines of his recently produced stage comedies.[6] Hofmannsthal, after *Ariadne*, had complimented himself on 'forcing a definite'[7] and beneficial style on Strauss; but now the boot was on the other foot. The composer, with fond memories of the strengths of *Rosenkavalier*, had now, after *Der Schwierige* and *Der Unbestechliche*, identified the nature of Hofmannsthal's genius and the direction in which its future lay, so far as their joint work was concerned.

A gentle flirtation with Viennese comedy had accompanied even the most esoteric phases of the poet's development. *Lucidor*, which in its earliest form was written in the year of *Der Rosenkavalier*'s inception (1909), was published as a sketch in Vienna in 1910, with the subtitle *Characters for an Unwritten Comedy*.[8] The tentative kinship with *Rosenkavalier* made *Lucidor*'s temporary abandonment after March 1911 virtually inevitable; but it never ceased to haunt Hofmannsthal's imagination, being taken up again in 1914 and in 1921, until being finally discarded in this first form in December 1922. In this brief but atmospheric story outline we see for the first time elements which moved through a diversity of forms over some sixteen years, but ultimately found their natural and proper place in the *Arabella* plans, which date from 1927. It can be summarised as follows:

The widow, Frau von Murska, after the sequestration of the family mansion (situated in the Russian sector of Poland), has brought her two daughters, Arabella and Lucile, to Vienna, where the family reside in an elegant hotel apartment overlooking the Kärntnerstraße. Arabella is by no means short of admirers due to the social pretensions of her mother, who considers Wladimir to be the most eligible. He has a good relationship with a mysterious rich uncle of the von Murskas, from whom the widow has certain expectation, and upon whose account she has chosen Vienna as a haven. Because the uncle cannot stand women at any price, she has persuaded Lucile to adopt the dress and manner of a youth, hoping that the uncle, recognising in Lucidor his only surviving apparently male relative, will advance his fortunes. Such a ruse has further advantages, for it relieves Frau von Murska of the expense of 'bringing out' two daughters, and also ensures that Lucile will present no threat to Arabella's matrimonial prospects. Arabella, however, shows little interest in Wladimir and, affronted by the fawning attentions showered upon him by her mother, encourages instead a certain Herr von Imfanger, with whom she pursues a coquettish affair. Her coldness towards her former swain drives him into a greater intimacy with the seeming Lucidor, whom, innocent of his true nature, he makes his confidant, and through whom he hopes to further his suit. The frustrated Lucile, trapped in her boyish disguise, soon falls deeply in love with Wladimir, and fearful that Arabella's heartlessness will drive him away, keeps his hopes alive by composing passionate love letters in her sister's handwriting. These letters require an unquestioning acceptance of Arabella's apparent public indifference and warn him that their sole method of communication must be through Lucidor. Through these letters and to Wladimir's great delight, Lucile arranges secret nightly assignations at which, under cover of darkness, she takes Arabella's place in blissful amorous encounters. Clearly, however, she is pursuing a path which can only end in disaster. In due course, the overstretched family finances, allied to the uncooperative attitude of the rich uncle, promote a situation which makes the von Murskas' departure from Vienna imminent. Distraught at the inevitability of losing her lover but helpless to intervene in her own destiny, Lucile sends him one final letter – setting a time for their last meeting, and bidding him adieu. Wladimir, however, is not prepared to give up Arabella so readily after the happiness he believes they have shared together. To Lucile's horror and Frau von Murska's great satisfaction, he insists on a meeting during the course of which, fearful of his ardour and outraged at his protestations, Arabella flees the room. As the astonished Wladimir, embarrassed and bewildered at her unequivocal denials, licks his wounds, the door opens to reveal a tearful Lucile dressed in one of her sister's nightgowns. The amazed Wladimir at once recognises his beloved: all is made clear to him at last; they pledge their love; the family fortunes are saved.

Despite obvious points of similarity with the later opera – Lucile's '*travestie*' role, family poverty, the expectation of a rich suitor for Arabella and Lucile's love for Wladimir – Hofmannsthal's notes also include a good deal of significant additional character and background material. Thus, we recognise in the rather foolish, scatterbrained Fràu von Murska, with her social pretensions and veneer of nobility, the prototype of Adelaide; just as Wladimir, by virtue of his wealth, aristocratic Balkan descent, courtship of Arabella and ultimate relationship with Lucile, hovers midway between the portrayals of Matteo and Elemer. It is nevertheless apparent that this early sketch, despite being released for publication by Hofmannsthal, is in no sense rounded and complete. Arabella herself appears only as a minor figure, while the roles of the rich uncle, the suitor Herr Imfanger, and the housekeeper are never properly explained or motivated. The sporadic jottings of later years did not contribute greatly to the overall coherence of the project. Apart from the obvious legacy of setting and period atmosphere, perhaps the most remarkable aspect of *Lucidor*, from the point of view of *Arabella*, is its preoccupation with the Lucile/Wladimir *motif* which helps considerably to elucidate the shrouded origins of the Zdenka/Matteo sub-plot of the later work.

Hofmannsthal's sources for *Lucidor* reflect as usual a wide range of cultural influences including elements from Dostoevsky's *The Idiot*, the Rosalind 'disguise' *motif* from Shakespeare's *As You Like It* and, perhaps most important of all, Molière's *Dépit amoureux*, from which the poet culled the central 'assignation' theme of the *dénouement*. With the passage of time and subsequent revision – intermittently between 1923 and 1927 as a film project, and later as a theatre Vaudeville entertainment for the actor Gustav Waldau – the plot of the earlier scenario was overlaid by new ideas and, stimulated by Hofmannsthal's friend C. J. Burkhardt, with psychological overtones, to the point where it retained small relationship to the original.

Hofmannsthal toyed with the *Lucidor* theme, on and off, from 1910 to 1927. During this period, which saw the production of *Rosenkavalier*, both versions of *Ariadne auf Naxos*, and *Die Frau ohne Schatten* as well as the bulk of the *Ägyptische Helena* text, Strauss's increasing pressure for a return tó the style of the earlier Viennese comedy – that 'second *Rosenkavalier*, without its mistakes and *longueurs!. . .*Something delicate, amusing and warm-hearted!'[9] – was a plea that, although work on *Helena* had only recently begun, struck a sympathetic chord in Hofmannsthal's mind. Just over a year later, in November 1924, he wrote:

When I allow my thoughts to rove beyond *Helena* and try to absorb your wish that we might succeed once again in producing something like *Rosenkavalier* (but not a copy of it!), then *Intermezzo. . .* provides the most exact cue for the line along which my imagination will have to travel and is certain to give me definite stimulus and inspiration. The work I took in hand a few days ago will perhaps show you, on the other hand, far better than anything else what I can do in my present state – fourteen years after *Rosenkavalier* – in the field towards which you wish to draw me. For last week I completed a tragedy in prose on which I have been working since 1920 and in order to relax from the strain, I have picked up one of the most lighthearted and attractive of my subjects, a Viennese comedy which I mean to put on the stage in the costume of the 1880's.[10]

The idea mooted here, *Der Fiaker als Graf* or *The Cabby as Count*, had been taken up in late August of that year and provided the second important fund of source material for *Arabella*.

The first known reference to this new work occurs in 1924, in a letter from Hofmannsthal to the theatre historian Max Pirker, a friend and colleague of Joseph Gregor, founder and director of the *Theatersammlung* of the Österreichische Nationalbibliothek.[11] The letter suggests that together they might examine a treatise on the early history of Viennese theatre by Alexander von Weilens, Gregor's predecessor at the Nationalbibliothek. The poet was also interested in a collection of *Volkskomödie* texts of the first half of the eighteenth century previously drawn to his attention by Pirker, who published them in 1927.[12] The intention was to trace a *Volksstück* entitled *Der Fiaker als Marquis*, by the early nineteenth-century Viennese popular dramatist, Adolf Bäuerle,[13] and to see 'Whether it might appropriately be used for a certain theatrical purpose'. The idea proved successful, and by November 1924 Hofmannsthal was well advanced with initial *Fiaker* sketches, of which he wrote to Joseph Gregor in a letter on the 17th of the month:

I finished *Der Turm* a few days ago and have at once switched over to a very different milieu, that of the lighter Viennese comedy, which, if it's successful, will weave together many threads – outstandingly from *Rosenkavalier* and from *Der Schwierige*. This backwards glance will however also take account of even older dramatic models.[14]

Despite his obvious fascination with the new *Fiaker* material, witnessed by a flurry of notes and preliminary drafts written through the following autumn and New Year, its development was cut short in February 1925, the date of his final sketches, in favour of a new tragedy, *Kaiser Phokas*, which he never finished. There was much else to occupy his time and energies, not least his concern about the future directorship of the Vienna Opera after Strauss's recent resignation.[15] Other distractions included work on the stage version of *Der Turm*, difficult editorial decisions over the projected publication of his correspondence with Strauss, and, most pressing, the additions and alterations to *Helena* which had, as composition reached the second and third acts, run into all kinds of difficulties.

It is not until 1927, after the completion of *Helena*, that a clearer picture emerges concerning the fate of the *Fiaker* comedy, which was once again taken up in October that year, this time in a more determined manner, helped by encouragement from the now restless and work-starved composer. Hofmannsthal's letter to Strauss of 1 October records the first real step towards the new *Arabella* project.

Two years ago I occupied myself with a comedy, made notes and drafted a scenario, and then I put this work aside again. It was called: *The Cabby as Count (Der Fiaker als Graf)*. (Please keep the title to yourself.) It was quite attractive as a subject, but in the end I found there was not enough to it if it was to be done in contemporary dress. The whole situation of the piece was still entirely true in my youth (so long as the court and aristocracy meant everything in Vienna); today it would have to be switched back in point of time: I did think of the eighteen-eighties or even of the eighteen-sixties. I was turning it over in my mind and as I did so another subject, a serious one, took hold of me and so I put the sketch into my drawer with all the rest. Last night it occurred to me that this comedy might perhaps be done for music, with the text in a light vein, largely in telegram style. The first act – as far as I recollect – will do; the second will be particularly suitable: it takes place in a ballroom and offers enchanting possibilities. The third act I can no longer remember very clearly. Now yesterday it occurred to me for the first time that the whole thing had a touch of *Rosenkavalier* about it, a most attractive woman as the central figure, surrounded by men, mostly young ones, a few episodes, too – no sort of outward likeness or similarity to *Rosenkavalier*, but an intimate affinity. But I cannot possibly give you, or even tell you any of it before January. To begin with I shall have to get my notes forwarded from Rodaun, where they are buried somewhere, and then the scenario for a light opera (in the *Rosenkavalier* style, but lighter still, still more French, if one can say that – still further removed from Wagner) will have to gain in substance in my mind. If the scenario pleases you, and if it pleases me too, getting the first act on to paper will be no great feat, for the style in which the libretto is to be done is already shaping in my imagination. . .Therefore, if you can muster enough patience, I take hope![16]

Hofmannsthal's interest in this idea stemmed naturally from an instinctive identification with his Viennese roots, as well as from a desire to reach a wider theatre-going public. In selecting such a subject he was tapping a rich, centuries-old traditional vein, represented, for modern non-Viennese audiences, by Emanuel Schikaneder, who wrote the *Lustspiel Die Zauberflöte* for Mozart in 1791.

The Viennese popular comedy, the *Volksstück*, evolving from the buffo *Hanswurst* elements established by Josef Anton Stranitzky in the early 1700s, had reached its high point at the start of the nineteenth century in the hands of artists of the calibre of Bäuerle, Josef Alois Gleich and Karl Meisl. The most celebrated of these actor/playwright/managers, Ferdinand Raimund, joined the Leopoldstadt Theater company in 1817, and the tradition was maintained in the next generation by the brilliantly gifted Johann Nepomuk Nestroy. The emphasis was upon comic entertainment – magic burlesque verging on pantomime, topically allusive and exploiting local character and dialect. The *Volksstück* was a medium which mirrored vividly the working-class Vienna of its day, reflecting its manners, humour, and way of life, as also its opinion of its masters. Hofmann-sthal's strongly developed historical perception, his consciousness of Austria's past, and his complicated, emotional involvement with his native city, were factors in this flirtation with the *Wiener Volkstradi-tion*. The *Fiaker* ethos, reminiscent of the harlequinade in *Ariadne*, also appealed through its racy atmosphere, its witty, free conversa-tional style, and the colourful traditional combination of song, music and dance elements, especially significant in view of the poet's commitment to Richard Strauss.

The *Fiaker* sketches themselves are not complete; moreover Hof-mannsthal also later admitted to finding the material too slight for independent development. It is impossible to glean more than an impression of the nature and argument of the piece, which owed little to Bäuerle save the title; and this, on grounds of historical credi-bility, Hofmannsthal soon altered to *Der Fiaker als Graf*. Bäuerle's play centres around a 'child substitution' *motif*, whereby a destitute mother attempts to safeguard her son's future by effecting a secret exchange with a scion of the nobility. The device is, in intent, re-miniscent of Frau von Murska's machinations in *Lucidor*; the per-ception may have forged a link in the poet's mind between the two scenarios, leading to their ultimate combination in *Arabella*.

In the event, Hofmannsthal drew his material from a whole tradi-tion of *Fiaker* farces which pre-dated Bäuerle, and reached back to the eighteenth century, in particular to the two plays, *Der Fiaker in Baden* and *Der Fiaker in Wien*, with which Schikaneder, at the *Theater an der Wien*, had attempted to rival the popularity of the *Leopoldstadt Theater* in 1793. It is also evident from allusions in Hofmannsthal's sketches that as with *Lucidor*, Molière had exerted an important, even critical influence upon the *Fiaker* plot with his *Les précieuses ridicules*, in which two counts, disappointed in love, seek revenge on their erstwhile sweethearts. Their men-servants, disguised as noblemen, win the affections of the ladies, presenting them at a court ball, where to their embarrassment a grand unmask-ing takes place. The *Fiaker* drafts abound in all manner of biblio-graphical references and allusions which, though they underline the breadth of Hofmannsthal's reading, and have generic interest, are tenuous in the extreme. Their value lies primarily in the insight they provide into the workings of a sophisticated creative mind – detailed investigation lies outside the province of this study.[17]

While the dramatic elements of *Der Fiaker als Graf* remain some-what indistinct, the central of the three proposed acts does foreshadow in its ballroom setting the second act of *Arabella*. Although it is not easy to follow the threads of Hofmannsthal's very personal and often apparently unconnected ideas, certain details emerge which have a counterpart in the later *Arabella* opera. Thus reference is made to Dominik, Lamoral and Matteo – finally even to Zdenka – as well as to others who find places in the earliest, and later discarded, libretto drafts. The most important of the *Fiaker* characters however is Emilie – or Milli, as she later became – on whose relationships to the young men who surround her the action of these sketches turns. Nevertheless, except for her working-class Viennese dialect, there is nothing in the text to link her directly with the flamboyant Fiakermilli of the opera, although it would be naïve to ignore the shared name of the historical Fiakermilli, Emilie Tureček, who lived from 1846 to 1889.

The Viennese *Fiaker*, or cab drivers, now a mere tourist attraction, were once a colourful feature of life in the Austrian capital. They formed a close-knit, racy and individual community, within the working class; their tradition, pride, dialect and humour were a byword. Hofmannsthal had innumerable sources for his knowledge of the *Fiaker* culture; but it is interesting to note that the Viennese music critic Ludwig Karpath, a long-standing friend of Strauss, and *au fait* with Hofmannsthal's *Arabella* proposals, enquired of Strauss in October 1928 if he should tell Hofmannsthal of a new source of 'Vienniana' he had discovered in the hands of the lawyer Dr Alfred Pick. Pick's collection included a mass of authentic information on the *Fiakerball* – newspaper cuttings etc. – which might interest the poet.[18] Karpath's intention was approved by Strauss, but there is no evidence that Hofmannsthal used this material, although Pick's observations, eventually published, constitute a useful account of the nature and character of the *Fiakerball* and thus of the general ambience that Hofmannsthal was attempting to create.

The visitor was assailed from every direction by an outpouring of Viennese music – song, popular ballad, waltz or march – sung, or piped by excellent military bands but above all performed by quartets of which the most outstanding from 1880 onward was the famous *Schrammelquartett*. The occasion promoted the appearance of professional artists, as well as the more ephemeral talents of popular singers, whilst ordinary members of the public – complete unknowns – would also join the musicians, who would be prevailed upon to accompany them in a song, a practice by means of which quite remarkable vocal talent was often discovered. Most of the 'numbers', however, would be rendered by the so-called *Natursänger*, whose unaffected popular sentimentality often 'brought the house down' and to whom no respite was granted. Social differences ceased to exist at the *Fiakerball*, which would be attended by listeners from all walks of life. Most of the participants, however, belonged to one of two main groups – the *Fiaker* community, or the very highest aristocratic circles. All *Fiakereigentümer* or cabowners were expected to bring their wives, daughters, sons and relatives, whilst amongst the aristocracy it was considered to be highest 'chic' to attend in evening dress, with decorations, and strictly without female company. It goes without saying that 'conviviality' was the order of the day, encouraged, no doubt, by the vast quantities of champagne which were drunk. The *Fiaker* also arrayed themselves in evening dress whilst their consorts were immaculately turned out in the most painstaking *Balltoiletten*. The first *Fiakerball* took place in 1787 out in the Viennese suburbs, but over the years the venue crept gradually closer and closer to the city centre until a decade later the event was taking place in the *Blumensäle*, an elegant restaurant on the *Ringstraße*. The balls were always held on Ash Wednesdays and reached their peak of popularity in the years between 1880 and 1900. Fiakermilli herself, Emilie Tureček, was twice married – the second time to one *Fiaker* Demel – and was active during that period when the *Fiakerball* reached the heights of its popularity. For a number of years the ball was held under her patronage and revolved around her personality which made such an impact that a virtual '*Milli*-cult' developed in Vienna.[19]

Friedrich Schlögl points out in a newspaper report of 1876 that eventually the *Fiakerbälle* were banned by the police because they tended to get out of control and were an offence to pious Christians during Lent.[20] The veto was overcome despite the authorities, and the balls were still held as 'private' functions at the houses of prominent members of *Fiaker* society.

Strauss and Hofmannsthal used considerable licence in their interpretation of the *Fiaker* elements in the *Arabella* scenario. Certainly the character of Fiakermilli with her yodelling refrain can be challenged – and was, by Strauss's supporter Clemens Krauss – on grounds of musical authenticity; while the ball scene itself has more sophistication and elegance than the *Fiaker* world to which the commentaries and researches of Schlögl and Pick introduce us. The presence of the Countess Adelaide and her daughter in the retinue of Waldner and Elemer offends against strict historical accuracy, but then the collaborators' decisions were primarily reached on musical and dramatic grounds. As far as Hofmannsthal was concerned, the *Fiaker milieu* was an animated and stylised concept upon which he could draw, and which he was free to transcend. The colourful, racy world of the 1860s was sufficiently remote in time, yet still a reality seen through the romantic mist of youth. It gives an intriguing and historically authentic fantasy-background against which the second act of *Arabella* is set. Hofmannsthal considered this act to be crucial to the dramatic viability of the work, through its establishment of the essential contrast between the restrictive salon elegance of *Lucidor*, and the uninhibited gaiety and freedom of the *Fiaker* world.

Of the characteristics which linked the sketches for *Lucidor* and *Der Fiaker als Graf*, perhaps the most significant was their historical period and dramatic setting. So far as the proposed opera was concerned, it was inevitable that the collaborators should seek to avoid too overt a comparison with *Rosenkavalier*, especially as the projected new comedy was initially conceived, albeit primarily in technical terms, as its successor. The advance in period between *Der Rosenkavalier* and *Arabella* of over a hundred years, from the 1740s to the 1860s, offered the latter a more accessibly realistic *milieu*, essentially different from that of its predecessor and peopled with a new range of characters inhabiting a changed social world. Equally important was the common setting, Vienna itself, particularly appropriate from Hofmannsthal's point of view, continuing the line of his previous Viennese 'conversational' comedies, *Der Schwierige* and *Der Unbestechliche*. Above all, it is the essential central element of disguise (whether translation of *Fiaker* into *Graf*, or Lucile into Lucidor), and the necessity for motivic dimension and dramatic contrast, that provides the ultimate spring of Hofmannsthal's action in combining these two embryo works.

By October 1927 the time was ripe for the first positive moves towards *Arabella*. Hofmannsthal had long ago set aside the *Fiaker* sketches, whose final drafts stem from February 1925, and which he considered too insubstantial for effective dramatic development. His interest in the *Lucidor* subject however had never waned, and as late as July 1927, anxious not to waste such promising material, he was actively promoting the film version that had first attracted him in December 1924.[21] It is clear that Hofmannsthal had an inner compulsion to find a dramatic outlet for *Lucidor*, and that Strauss's promptings also played their part in keeping the project in his mind. It is easy to understand why when Strauss suggested Turgenev's *Smoke*,[22] Hofmannsthal ignored the subject but seized upon the setting – the 1860s: 'The costume of this period, it is true, would appeal to me greatly. Perhaps this suggestion contains the germ of something one might be able to do after all!'[23]

This accords with what we already know of Hofmannsthal's preoccupation with *Lucidor*; but it is less easy to understand why

Strauss, replying a few days later, touches 'out of the blue' once again on that long abandoned *Fiaker* work:

I read that you are working on a *Wiener Volkstheater*. Wouldn't that make an operatic text too some day, or a *Singspiel* with music (and a Punch and Judy show), or even a spoken popular play with musical interludes and ballet à la Molière?[24]

Unquestionably, the date of this letter is correct, so it would be interesting to know just what prompted Strauss to make so fateful a comment at this moment. Less than two weeks later, and just as unexpectedly,[25] Hofmannsthal explicitly and for the first time made the important link between *Lucidor* and *Der Fiaker als Graf*. Was it, one wonders, that apparently random remark of Strauss's that, jogging his memory and stimulating his imagination, prompted him to cast his mind back to the *Der Fiaker* drafts of 1925, and to reassess their potential – as a dramatic foil to *Lucidor* – for the new collaboration? A month later, on 13 November 1927, Hofmannsthal was able to write:

Although I am wholly engrossed in a new dramatic piece of work, I have sent for the notes to *Der Fiaker als Graf* and for the sketches of several other comedies besides. *Der Fiaker als Graf* was intended as a spoken play, depending entirely on its dialogue; the action, in so far as one can speak of action at all, was too flimsy for an opera. But I have been able to combine several features of this cabbies' world with elements from another projected comedy and hope (I may still find myself mistaken, but I hope!) to have invented the scenario for a three-act comic opera, indeed almost an operetta (I would describe *Rosenkavalier* as an operetta too!), which in gaiety does not fall short of *Fledermaus*, is kindred to *Rosenkavalier*, without any self-repetition, and contains five or six very lively parts, above all a very strong second act and a third which does not in any way fall off.[26]

Here at last we see evidence of the evolution of 'the little comic opera or musical comedy', with which, as Hofmannsthal said, 'We are going to challenge *Rosenkavalier*'.[27] By 20 November, he was able to assure Strauss, in a mood of the highest expectation, that

The characters of this new comedy for music are cutting their capers under my very nose, almost too obtrusively. The spirits which I summoned for your sake now refuse to leave me alone. The comedy might turn out better than *Rosenkavalier*. . .Perhaps I shall be able to offer you once more, as I did seventeen years ago, something which lends itself to easy-flowing creative labour.[28]

4 *The Arabella collaboration*

Once the conceptual link between *Lucidor* and *Der Fiaker als Graf* had been forged in November 1927,[1] the collaboration moved very fast. This was to be the work with which, as Hofmannsthal said, 'We are going to challenge *Rosenkavalier*',[2] and Strauss, already putting the finishing touches to *Die ägyptische Helena*, and desperate to avoid a barren period, spurred on his librettist with enthusiastic encouragement. By the middle of December, they had met in Vienna to discuss Hofmannsthal's proposals, which even at this stage included the Croatian landowner Mandryka, a figure entirely unforeshadowed in the contributory sources, who nevertheless enables these two dissimilar but complementary sketch designs to be amalgamated. It was at Aussee towards the end of October that Hofmannsthal developed the first tentative outline of the new *Fiaker* scenario; it appears that the Mandryka character, and the link with *Lucidor*, evolved during working sessions with his friend, the writer R. A. Schröder, early in November.[3] A week or two of hard thinking and working crystallised the main elements of the plot, and added and defined a number of important subsidiary roles; so that on 20 November, after admitting a fascinated preoccupation with these 'Spirits which I summoned up for your sake', Hofmannsthal could write to Strauss:

The comedy might turn out better than *Rosenkavalier*. The figures have taken a very distinct shape in my mind and offer excellent contrasts. The two girls (sopranos) could develop into magnificent (singing) parts. . .As lovers a high tenor and a baritone. This latter is the most remarkable character in the piece, from a semi-alien world (Croatia), half buffo and yet a grand fellow capable of deep feelings, wild and gentle, almost daemonic.[4]

The working notes demonstrate that by the mid-December meeting the general shape of the first act was clear in Hofmannsthal's mind, as well as most of the important dramatic elements of the second. This latter, together with jottings for the third act, existed at that time only in very rudimentary form, but nonetheless included preliminary references to Fiakermilli; to Zdenka's assignation with Matteo; and also a transcription of the second act Slav folk-ballad which gives a degree of 'ethnic' authenticity to the Croatian Mandryka. These initial drafts fuelled a collaborative dialogue that continued up to 3 May 1928, by which date the composer had received a typescript of Act 1 in its first established form. At this stage in its development, the action still retained elements from the earlier *Fiaker* sources which were, perhaps regrettably, as the project evolved, written out of the score. These traces of Hofmannsthal's 'Volkstheater' concept not only included Nazi (from the original sketches) instead of Matteo, but also the introduction of *Fiaker* pseudonyms – 'Der Pinogl', 'Der Ungar', 'Der Weißfisch', 'Der Fux-mundihansel' and 'Der Sandor' – for the suitor-count 'cabbie' disguises of the first act masquerade – an authentically racy inspiration which might have contributed effectively to the variety, colour, and humour of the festive final scenes of the second act.[5]

With the creation of Mandryka, however, Hofmannsthal had achieved, as he himself realised, an innovative masterstroke. The blunt yet not ignoble rusticity of this character, contrasted with the mannered sophistication of Viennese society, had classic humorous potential – at the same time pointing the contrast between his peasant honesty and the corruption and intrigue of the *Kaiserstadt*. Furthermore, the implicit elevation of Arabella, whose choice he inevitably is, above the machinations of her fortune-hunting contemporaries invests her with the dramatically essential idealism of a heroine. The archetype of the rich landowner from the provinces would have been familiar to one whose youth and early manhood had been spent in late nineteenth-century Habsburg Vienna. Indeed, that glittering, decadent, childhood world, in which the personages of *Arabella* move, exercised a nostalgic attraction fundamental to Hofmannsthal's choice of material, background and period.

It is hardly surprising that Hofmannsthal's exultation in alighting on this original and prepossessing figure should have caused him to over-emphasise its significance to Strauss – leading him to believe, contrary to his own instinctive needs, that this role was to dominate the action. That assumption, prompting some nervous backward glances at *Rosenkavalier*'s Baron Ochs, certainly motivated Strauss's initial criticisms. In particular, he was fearful that Hofmannsthal's enthusiasm for this role would tempt him to exaggerate its importance at the expense of the female lead:

So far as I can pass any considered judgement after no more than a cursory acquaintance with your draft, it seems to me that you are again making the mistake that led you, as the loving author, to over-estimate the theatrical effect of Ochs von Lerchenau. . .The character which. . .ensured the final victory for *Rosenkavalier* is the Marschallin: her meditations about time, the passage about the clocks, the parting – and this is what seems to me to be lacking in the new subject. Your Croatian. . .wouldn't draw a hundred people into the theatre. . .This new piece, so far as I can judge it at this stage, lacks a genuinely interesting female character. The two daughters don't seem to me to fit the bill sufficiently.[6]

In an ill-conceived attempt to redress the balance, Strauss toyed with the idea of giving more prominence to Adelaide, suggesting a flirtation between her and Arabella's suitors, or even a prior entanglement with 'the mysterious Croatian gentleman'. Fortunately, both partners realised that such a development would inevitably result in the creation of a 'sham Marschallin', as Hofmannsthal was quick to point out, 'a damaging improvement!'[7]

Hofmannsthal's attitude was positive and reassuring – 'Your sense of the theatre and of life is completely right. The central figure must be a woman, and not the baritone.'[8] It had always been his intention that Arabella's position in the drama should be pre-eminent. He had, from the outset, he maintained, envisaged her as 'A thoroughly mature, wide awake young girl conscious of her strength and of the hazard she runs, completely mistress of the situation. . .an entirely modern character', adding that 'Such intelligent and self assured young girls are Bernard Shaw's best figures; his St Joan is one of them.'[9] He was quick to point out that Mandryka was never intended to be the leading figure, any more than was Ochs in *Rosenkavalier*, but rather 'The personage who, by his very entrance, by his arrival from the country into an alien world, sets the action going'.[10]

For all Strauss's reservations, he grasped the musical opportunities offered by the Mandryka role. He had, with typical enthusiasm, plunged into a study of Southern Slavonic folk song with the express intention of 'knocking up a colossal Croatian ballet for our second act',[11] a suggestion that alarmed Hofmannsthal:

slight nuances of this kind in colour and in rhythm can greatly benefit this particular figure, but of course only this particular figure, that Croatian gentleman. . .It would be appalling if [it] were to become a music box for Croat folk tunes. . .Your reference to a ballet, or indeed to a 'colossal ballet' founded on a South Slav air has somewhat horrified me. For heaven's sake! Here I shall have to make a firm stand, for it is exactly the decisive point that everything must be authentic, the authentic Vienna of 1860, just as *Rosenkavalier* owes some part of its success to the fact that it is throughout the authentic Vienna of 1740. Therefore: we are at the Vienna Cabbies' Ball and on such an occasion there can be no more question of a Croatian dance than of a Persian or an Indian one. [12]

As he points out, whilst the *Lucidor* 'theme' had haunted him for years, he had always believed the action too slight to stand on its own. Suddenly, with the development of the Arabella/Mandryka *motif,* the whole concept had become viable at last. The new main plot, he stresses, centres around

a distinct, very pregnant situation for Arabella. She is a mature and beautiful girl who has probed deeply into certain aspects of life, a little seared by cynicism and resignation, she is ready to enter into an arid *mariage de convenance* (with a man who never appears on the stage at all). For this girl the most unlikely suitor now turns up out of the blue. And the same flash of imagination revealed to me the figure of this suitor: a most picturesque personality composed of many attractive qualities (and what is more a *singing* figure). So what was before the main motif (the Zdenka/Matteo plot) receded into the background and from now on functions merely to motivate the action as an element of suspense (and very happily at that); a suspense which is resolved only in the third act. [13]

At this stage, no doubt happy at the prospect of a successor to *Helena,* Strauss allowed events to take their natural course, resisting the temptation to hustle his librettist towards a solution. Indeed, the interim correspondence, prior to delivery of the first completed working draft of Act 1, demonstrates untypical restraint on Strauss's part. One should bear in mind that from January to April 1928 both artists were based in Vienna, Hofmannsthal being currently occupied with the opening night of *Der Turm* in February, and both crucially involved with preparations for the pending *Helena* premiere which was scheduled for June. At all events, there would have been opportunity for personal discussion before Strauss's departure from Vienna on 18 April, by which time Hofmannsthal, after concentrated and detailed organisation of the *Arabella* material, had demonstrated his own commitment to the work. Commenting on the variety of mood and action in the first act, which, he asserts, strikes him as the best he has ever written, he hails it as 'a real exposition', arousing interest for what is to come and introducing all the characters of the drama. [14]

Progress during subsequent months resulted in a clearer general outline and in the emergence of coherent sectional workings. While the overall structure of the act is still somewhat hesitant, the essential dramatic shape of the whole work is seen to be emerging. For all that, the end result demonstrates both diffuseness and periodicity, and as Strauss later commented, for all its strengths, lacked sufficient organisational integration for his purpose. Scene by scene, it may be summarised as follows (dramatic detail is only supplied in scenes which differ substantially in content from the final version of the text: sequences of events ultimately carried forward into the libretto of the opera are noted in square brackets):

(1) Creditors/Zdenka: their demands confirm her fears of the family's imminent departure from Vienna and her inevitable separation from Matteo.

(2) Zdenka/Matteo: [His hopes for a letter. Jealous questions about Arabella]

(3) Zdenka/Adelaide: the latter bewails the family misfortunes. Zdenka pleads to be allowed to cast off her disguise but is reminded that the Fortune-teller prophesied a rich marriage for Arabella, who must be allowed a clear field. Adelaide gloats over the attentions of the three counts, Elemer, Dominik and Lamoral, whom Zdenka scornfully derides – Matteo alone is worthy of her sister's love.

(4) Arabella enters and springs at once to her sister's defence, asserting her right to abandon this 'Cinderella' role. She declares that her own destiny (marriage with a rich building contractor who has been pursuing her) will be decided after the *Faschingszeitball* that very evening.

(5) Adelaide/Waldner: [Desperate financial situation – Mandryka/ Arabella plans – portrait – need for rich marriage at all costs] Mandryka's servants, Welko and Jankel, reconnoitre the situation from the doorway.

(6) Adelaide/Waldner/Arabella/Zdenka/The Counts: the last-named now present themselves. In 'cabby' disguise they bear gifts for Arabella – a masquerade-like invitation for her to preside as queen of the *Faschingsball*. Matteo has also put in an appearance and, appalled to find the Counts in his way again, voices his annoyance to an equally irritated Zdenka. The hotel refuses to serve refreshments unless the family's outstanding bills are paid but Arabella saves further embarrassment by dismissing her suitors, promising to meet them later for an afternoon drive.

(7) In desperation, Waldner now instructs Adelaide to pawn the Count's gifts, but his wife still clings hopefully to the gipsy's prophecy, which Arabella, who has already decided her course of action, dismisses as romantic nonsense.

(8) Waldner/Mandryka: [Bitter reflection on Arabella's sacrifice – arrival of Mandryka – his wooing – offers financial aid to Waldner]

(9) Waldner/Adelaide/Arabella: he seeks an opportunity to present Mandryka but her afternoon commitments defer introductions until the evening's ball.

(10) Arabella/Zdenka/Matteo: Arabella retires to an adjoining room to write the letter which must be sent to the wealthy building contractor accepting his marriage offer. Zdenka is distraught, and when Matteo unexpectedly appears enjoins silence, explaining that her sister is within earshot. She leads Matteo to believe that the letter Arabella is writing is destined for him – all will be explained, including the reasons for Arabella's erratic behaviour, at

the ball that evening. Matteo implores her to keep faith, and hurriedly departs.

(11) Zdenka is completely overcome – all hope is gone. If only she could express to him the love she feels – but it is Arabella's words he wants, not hers – she might as well drown herself. Arabella returns – it is time to get dressed for the afternoon drive. As she joins her sister, she calls in anguish for God to pity her. The curtain falls.[15]

Even in this early draft, one recognises many points of similarity with the plan that Strauss and Hofmannsthal ultimately adopted for this act. Scenes 2, 5 and 8, remained essentially unchanged throughout the entire collaboration. Elsewhere – notably in scenes 6 and 11 – certain individual *motifs* were to become transposed in order and context, with others being either dramatically highlighted, refined or discarded.

Strauss's receipt of a draft based upon the above scheme early in May 1928 initiated a new stage in the collaboration, reactivating his critical faculties and culminating in Hofmannsthal's important textual revisions of July 1928. At first sight, Strauss pronounced the draft 'on the whole splendid', particularly admiring the 'three-dimensional' nature of the main characters, but still admitting reservations about that of Arabella, which he described as 'rather vague in outline' and at times 'insignificant and ordinary' in expression. Whilst the overall concept appealed strongly to him, 'Warmest congratulations. . .I'm having high hopes of the remainder!' – he felt that the planning, from the end of scene 8 onwards, left much to be desired. This, he maintained, was the classic position for an ensemble, a quintet perhaps, which would sum up the aspirations of each of the main characters. He also criticised the piecemeal nature of the Zdenka/Matteo scenes (2, 6 and 10), which could, he believed, be effectively condensed. Above all, the final curtain, rather than being left to two subsidiary characters (Zdenka and Matteo) – 'pretty but not effective – would definitely have to conclude with the solo voice, an aria, a lyrical outpouring from Arabella'.[16]

It is symptomatic of the understanding which now existed between the collaborators that Hofmannsthal, nothing daunted by Strauss's comments, was able to comply promptly with his requests. By 13 July, he had sent instructions to Strauss to cut out Matteo's involvement in Scene 6, written and inserted the material for the ensemble in Scene 8,[17] and recast the finale of the act which now appears in its penultimate form:

Arabella, in full view of the audience but concealed from the adjoining

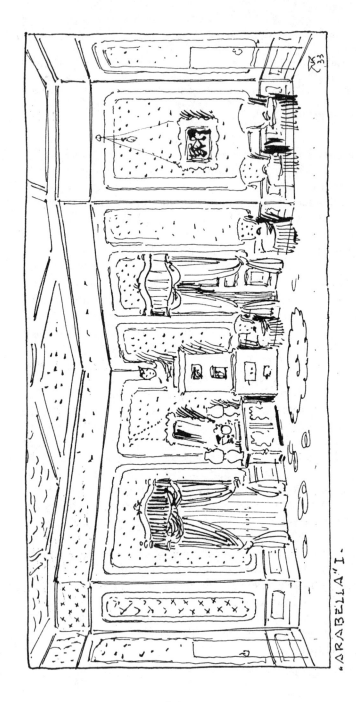

"ARABELLA" I.

7 Scene sketch (Alfred Roller): Act 1, Viennese *Arabella* premiere, October 1933. The set for Act 2 was, on economic grounds, pirated from the ball scene of Heuberger's operetta *Ein Opernball.*

onstage room, is about to write her acceptance of the building contractor's offer of marriage. Zdenka warns Matteo, who has joined her in the salon, to speak softly – her sister is close at hand. As Arabella reflects on the consequences of her decision, so Zdenka comforts Matteo, encouraging him to believe that the letter her sister writes is that which he has so long and impatiently awaited. The grim realities of her situation dawn afresh upon Arabella. Her oft-admired charms, she reflects, seem not to be destined for the man of her dreams, who, if he exists at all, has been unable to find his way to her. She asks God's protection as she faces the decision that has been forced upon her. Meanwhile Zdenka fends off Matteo's anxious enquiries; the letter is, as yet, unfinished; he will receive it later that evening. He exits, abjuring her to keep faith. Despairingly, she commits her cause to God; her heart alone is full of love for Matteo, but to no avail. Arabella re-enters; the letter is finished. It will seal her destiny. As she, in anguish, calls upon heaven for aid, so her optimistic nature re-asserts itself; tomorrow is another day! Soon it will be the *Faschingsball*; now sleighs await in the street: with delight she reflects on the evening's festivities over which she is to reign as queen.[18]

It is clear that elements of this revision reappear in the ultimate 'Mein Elemer' *finale* of July 1929. The new draft, a vast improvement over the original, also went some way towards correcting the imbalance in the Arabella role. But this, together with an overall deficiency in the psychological motivation of the act, still worried Strauss, who now (July 1928), on receipt of a sketch outline for the remainder of the work, instigated further changes which would, he hoped, rectify the situation. 'I know you'll be horrified at first, because my suggestion knocks half your opera into a heap', he commented to Hofmannsthal, 'But Acts II and III, thank God, are still only in draft. Once you've accepted my ideas the alterations won't give you too much trouble.'[19]

Planning for the succeeding acts had, in fact, progressed simultaneously with the more detailed compilation of Act 1, the second bearing a close resemblance to the completed text up to the moment of Zdenka's gift of the key to Matteo, and the third conforming in outline as far as the beginning of the final scene. Here Adelaide leads Arabella down the staircase to Mandryka, while Djura, his gipsy servant, accompanies their betrothal with 'nightingale sounds' on his fiddle. This latter twist, to which Strauss objected, 'it reeks strongly of Lehar',[20] was soon abandoned; but the ceremony of the betrothal drink, which Strauss thought too like the already heavily criticised magic potions of *Helena*, Hofmannsthal was rightly determined to retain, not least on dramatic grounds.

Instead of any ceremony at this point, one could of course have the still outstanding engagement kiss. Yet this simple ceremony of carrying the filled glass down the stairs, has immense mimic advantages. A kiss she cannot *carry towards him*. . .the other [the ceremony] implies the most bridal gesture in its chastest form, and it can be followed by the kiss which thus gains solemnity, something that raises it out of the ordinary: from this final moment after such a lot of fracas I expect much.[21]

Of the three acts, the third was in fact the one least 'improved' or altered up to its final despatch to Strauss, together with a revision of the second (the fruit of Hofmannsthal's autumn labours), on 12 December 1928. It was Act 2 which had occupied most of his attention during the preceding months, for he had found himself unable to proceed with the music for Act 1 until the form of its successor had been finally decided. Under pressure from the composer Hofmannsthal now added a new scene for Arabella and Matteo to be inserted early in the first act (between scenes 2 and 3, above), designed to reveal a prior, amorous relationship between them.[22] This new *motif*, the sacrifice by Arabella of her love for Matteo in an attempt to restore the family fortunes, would, it was hoped, add credibility to Matteo's love for her, and generally heighten the dramatic conflict. In practice, the device merely anticipated Arabella's renunciation (in favour of the building contractor), as it then stood in the revised first act finale (quoted above) – surely one important reason why this extra scene was eventually discarded! It remains a genuine, albeit clumsy and in the event abortive, attempt to repair a psychological inconsistency in the action, a problem that was never satisfactorily resolved.

There is a good deal to support Strauss's opinion that Act 2 as it stood in the summer of 1928, was 'devoid of all real conflict'. Both men realised the need, after the expository first act, for a really dramatic climax involving all the main characters, which would depend upon the events of the final act for resolution. As usual, it was Strauss, with his acute theatrical sense and realistically bold approach, who put his finger on the problem, reminding the poet of a notable parallel, the 'famous' instance, where in the *Rosenkavalier* second act, his practical, hard-headed intervention had once saved the dramatic situation.[23] The earlier drafts correspond in outline to the completed text as far as Zdenka's delivery, to Matteo, of the key to Arabella's room. Thereafter, dramatically speaking, the piece 'hangs fire' – the original plan standing as follows:

Zdenka and Matteo leave, while at a side-table Mandryka, very elegant, sings a Serbian ballad and entertains Adelaide and Waldner to refreshments. After Arabella's farewells to Dominik and Elemer, Mandryka, elated at his good fortune, orders champagne and convivially acquaints Adelaide with a Slavonic betrothal custom which should be enacted on the engagement evening – that glass of spring water is worth all the champagne in the world! Arabella, meanwhile, takes tender leave of Lamoral before whisking him away to join the dancing guests. Wishing to be alone, she decides to retire for the night and, lest Mandryka misconstrue her action, writes him an explanatory note. He accepts her excuses cheerfully – in his eyes, she can do no wrong. Adelaide, however, reminds him of the need to perform the betrothal ceremony before the evening comes to an end – Arabella will not yet be asleep; they must all return to the hotel. Mandryka orders more champagne for the guests and jubilantly departs with Adelaide and Waldner, to ratify his engagement.[24]

Strauss saw at once what was needed to revitalise this uneventful plan, his observations proving 'of real service' to Hofmannsthal, who added, 'Your line of development for Act 2 convinces me at first sight. . .you cannot direct my imagination into more welcome channels.'[25] The new proposals, in which we clearly recognise the salient features of the opera's '*Fiakerball* finale, were suggested by Strauss in his letter of 8 August 1928:

At the beginning no dance music: only the various entrances (without chorus, without Fiaker-Milli), only Waldner, Adelaide (possibly with Arabella's three Counts), Mandryka. Arabella's first encounter with Mandryka – of which I don't like Arabella's alarm and sudden anxiety to leave: it strikes me as a bit trivial. Conversation Arabella–Mandryka, betrothal, as far as Arabella: '*Jetzt geben Sie mich eine Stunde frei*', etc. – At this point I would start a waltz in the orchestra and let it run on (as at the end of Act 2 of *Fledermaus*), and into this continuous waltz I should now like to fit: Arabella's leave-taking scene with the three Counts, the scene Matteo–Zdenka. . .and possibly a passing flirtation between Adelaide and one of the Counts – all of these as separate ensembles. . .at two separate tables. . . Next Mandryka's outburst of despair, at the same time frenzied climax of the ball, entrance of Fiaker-Milli amidst homage, now perhaps Mandryka's Slav song, equivocal, a blend of love, jealousy, desperate gaiety: exit Arabella with the whole ensemble, end of the waltz. Mandryka left alone, desperate: Arabella's note, confirmation of her unfaithfulness – scene between Fiaker-Milli and Mandryka, abruptly cut off at its climax (kiss) by Adelaide and Waldner: 'Where's Arabella?' 'Gone? We must go home', the betrothal, the glass of water – sudden awakening of Mandryka: home! Arabella! Tragic end!. . .The act would open with a ceremonial beginning, turn tenderly amorous, in the middle the great waltz as climax, then passion and despair, and an abrupt end as a thrilling transition to the developments and denouements of Act 3. Would this shape suit you?[26]

Hofmannsthal now proceeded to recast the act along these lines. Justifying his treatment of the Arabella/Mandryka meeting on grounds of her natural shyness and vulnerability, and rejecting the

Jankel 'spy' concept,[27] he yet manages, successfully sweeping aside some later grossly exaggerated proposals, to incorporate the remainder of the composer's suggestions into his plans. Rationalising Mandryka's apparently out-of-character 'snooping', he comments that 'Matteo must long for that final letter. . .but must fear it even more, because it is likely to be the last farewell. Thus he shrinks from Zdenka and she has to run after him to force the letter on him.' 'This incident', he continues, 'is so striking that Mandryka, who is no eavesdropper, finds himself intrigued by these goings-on and in stepping forward overhears the words: "It is the key to Arabella's room."'[28] It was precisely this new strand of psychological motivation that led, with Mandryka's jealous anger, to the more effective second act conclusion which embodied his drunken flirtation with Fiakermilli, his rudeness to the Waldners and his willingness to believe in the apparent perfidy of his sweetheart.

Following delivery of the last two acts of the opera to Garmisch, the collaborators again met in Vienna,[29] to review the entire situation. Although apparently satisfied with achievements so far, Strauss soon voiced new reservations, particularly in relation to the first act, with which he had never been entirely happy. The onstage appearance of the Fortune-teller had emanated from their post-Christmas discussions, but Strauss now proposed further adjustments. These, inevitably designed to ensure that the action was concentrated upon Arabella, harked back to earlier demands for a conclusion 'definitely with a solo voice, an aria, a lyrical outpouring from Arabella',[30] a substitute for the existing, and in Strauss's opinion somewhat ineffective, 'letter writing' *finale*.

During the early months of 1929, happy and willing to accede to Strauss's request, Hofmannsthal redoubled his efforts to locate Arabella at the centre of the drama. It was at this stage that her wistful account of an attractive stranger at the street corner was 'written in' to Act 1, a felicitous stroke which adds piquancy and depth to her character, and helps to prepare for and to rationalise her subsequent abrupt submission to Mandryka's passion. A more radical alteration involved the abandonment of the first act 'cabby' masquerade, 'difficult, if not impossible to understand outside Vienna',[31] now replaced by the existing fourth scene of the opera in which Elemer makes his over-confident bid for Arabella's affections. It was Hofmannsthal's intention, by excluding the three Counts at this juncture, to give prominence to this character in 'a strong (lyrical) scene' which would focus clearly upon Arabella, and 'help to lay the main

emphasis on Elemer's leave-taking',[32] during the threefold farewells
of Act 2.

Without doubt, Hofmannsthal believed that he had now met
Strauss's requirements in this respect, pointing out that 'The scenes
dominated by Arabella fill two thirds of the Act', placing her 'more
definitely in the centre, to throw her into every possible relief'.[33]
Nevertheless, to some extent he had 'begged the question', having, as
yet, failed to meet Strauss's wishes over the recasting of the first act
finale. This, which in its already once revised 'quasi-ensemble' form
had given him considerable pleasure, he was clearly reluctant to dis-
card. Given Strauss's dissatisfaction, and his dogged persistence in
the matter, it comes as no surprise when, in a survey, on 6 July, accepting his librettist's overall plan for the act with obvious relief, he
repeats his previous requests emphatically:

Arabella must at all costs conclude the first act with a longish aria, soliloquy,
contemplation, if only for dramatic reasons. . .Contents of the soliloquy
something like this: she sits down to write a farewell letter to Matteo, inter-
spersed with recollections of her scene with Elemer, of her first encounter
with Mandryka – comparisons, vacillation, etc. . .The Arabella curtain as it
was before was also much too short and abrupt. In a three act opera the
first curtain, in particular, must be very effective, I am therefore asking you
urgently to arrange the whole act in such a manner that it moves with a com-
pulsive inevitability towards this lyrical solo scene of Arabella.[34]

This was on Friday 6 July 1929 – on the following Tuesday the Ms. of
the revised act, now including the beautiful concluding 'Mein Elemer'
solo, but omitting the early Arabella/Matteo scene and the quartet
ensemble, accompanied a final acquiescence from the poet:

Such a quiet contemplative close had been my objective, but I was uncertain
whether this would be what you want. Your letter, therefore, took a load off
my mind. I have done my best, especially in the scene between the two sisters,
to provide transitions from the dialogue into the lyrical mood at several
points – for Arabella alone, as well as for the two sisters together. What else
I have tried to do I have told you in my last letter.[35]

Four days later, Franz Hofmannsthal committed suicide – and on
Sunday 15 July 1929, Hofmannsthal himself, a few hours before his
son's funeral, suffered a heart attack and died. Unopened on his
desk lay a telegram from Garmisch, setting a seal of approval on the
labours of the preceding months, 'First Act excellent, many thanks
and congratulations, Richard Strauss'.[36]

The whole tenor of the correspondence between 1927 and 1929
suggests that these *Arabella* years belong, with those of *Der Rosen-*

kavalier, to one of the most congenial and mutually productive periods in a unique partnership. Strauss's practical nature can be seen very clearly at work, directing the action at every point and in the most minute detail. Equally noticeable is Hofmannsthal's aristocratic artistic refinement which vetoes anomalies such as Croatian dances in a Viennese ballroom, or stubbornly defends certain psychological twists of dialogue whose subtlety seems to have escaped the composer's comprehension. Hofmannsthal never loses his temper: despite the composer's occasionally outspoken comments, their free exchange of views, governed by the motto, 'Immune to offence in matters of art',[37] never seriously threatens equilibrium and objectivity. One observes in Hofmannsthal an increasingly reflective mood, less passionately self-protective than in earlier years. Apparently ever prepared to accede to Strauss's demands, he is involved in constant revision right to the end, free from rancour or concern, even though the additional labour must have cost him dear. Certainly, throughout this whole episode the poet's health was an increasing source of anxiety to himself and to those around him; and his acquiescence, primarily based on a well-founded confidence in his partner's shrewdness, also seems to reflect a weariness of spirit already looking forward to the *fin de siècle* nostalgia of Viennese decline which the opera portrays.

The impact of Hofmannsthal's death upon Strauss cannot be measured, personally or professionally. 'I still cannot comprehend it or lend words to my grief. It is too terrible', he mourned, 'a frightful blow to the entire world of art.'[38] So far as *Arabella* is concerned, one must be thankful that after so much revision, the first act had reached completion – but what of the other two? True, Strauss had already received the 'finished' manuscript, detailed knowledge of which was essential to enable him to finalise the shape of the expository first act. This demanding task had necessarily taken preference over all else, from December 1928 up to the poet's death, whilst the remainder of the work, for the time being, had to wait. There can be no doubt that this material, which had already undergone general 'planning' changes concurrently with its textual working, would also have been subjected to much more detailed revision if Hofmannsthal had lived. In the event, bemused and disorientated by the tragedy, Strauss sought an antidote in work, paying homage to his dead librettist by refusing to consider alterations, setting the text as far as possible in the 'completed' form in which the 'unforgettable friend'[39] had left it – as he confided to Anton Kippenberg, 'It is Hofmannsthal's last bequest, one has no choice but to execute it.'[40]

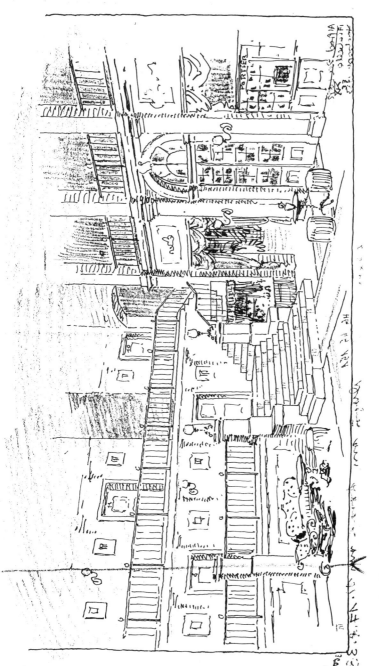

8 Scene sketch (Alfred Roller): Act 3 Viennese *Arabella* premiere, October 1933. It is of particular interest since the traversing line to the left was added by Strauss himself, to indicate the practical limits of the stage set.

A summary of the events leading up to the *Arabella* premiere does not belong here – it suffices to point out that after his tragic loss Strauss was sustained by the sympathy and encouragement of his friends in his efforts to bring the opera to completion. Fritz Busch and the Dresden *Intendant* Alfred Reucker, to whom the opera was to be jointly dedicated, were particularly supportive. A somewhat fitful progress, congenially interrupted by a Mozart reworking for Clemens Krauss, and prospects of a new composable text from Stefan Zweig, saw the final touches put to the score on 12 October 1933 – the last rites of a fruitful and unique artistic collaboration.

5 *The structure of the opera*

Structural responsibility in opera is not the prerogative of the music alone, although as the ultimate factor which determines and interprets the emotional shape of the drama, its importance is unassailable. The initial constructional impulse must stem from the libretto, whose formative influence is twofold: it evokes a stimulating creative ambience, and must also provide a dramatic framework for the musical ideas with which it will eventually be clothed. For Strauss and Hofmannsthal, the collaborative goal was specific and transcendent – 'To do something universally significant in the cultural sense by creating for once a flawless work of art'[1] – the attempt to achieve a balance between 'words' and 'music' taking place within the broader context of a mutually fertilising musical and literary design. Given their individuality and comparable artistic stature, it could hardly have been otherwise. What primarily concerns us is the extent to which they succeeded in reconciling the distinct, though not always dissimilar, technical requirements of the musical and dramatic structure of the work, for it is this which determines the significance of their achievement.

Keenly aware of the challenge which faced them, the authors of *Der Rosenkavalier* set out on their twelfth collaborative project. Now, as they turned, one feels with some relief, from the obscurity and allegorical remoteness of *Die Frau ohne Schatten* and *Helena*, the operetta 'dream' which had struggled so long for expression was close to realisation. 'I do believe that the style of the whole thing is well suited to yield something new. I consider it my chief obligation towards you that nothing I do should in style resemble too closely anything already done',[2] wrote Hofmannsthal – and this 'something new', we may infer, was an attempt through clear uncomplicated 'action', warm human interest and situational reality, to transpose some of the subtleties of spoken comedy directly onto the operatic stage.

63

It was inevitable, and also the major strength of the collaboration, that each project should be approached afresh from the separate standpoint of poet and composer. It was exactly this diversity of approach, leading to an already manifest ability to solve the problems of one medium in terms of the other, that gave the ultimate stamp of artistic quality to their joint efforts. The prime condition of the partnership had always been that the individual artistic freedom of each participant should be respected. Hofmannsthal's instinctive aim, to transfer the poetic subtleties and refined sentiment of his earlier prose comedies into opera, was apparent to Strauss. On receipt of the Act 1 draft, he immediately pointed out the need for 'more precise shape and clearer utterance', maintaining that 'For a spoken comedy the present form would no doubt be adequate; but for an opera, where so much text is inevitably lost, the outline is too delicate.'[3] 'Yes, the danger to be avoided is this', conceded the poet, 'I must take care not to come too close to spoken comedy!'[4]

It was this over-subtlety of motivation and 'piecemeal' episodic construction, 'impossible to forge into an integrated musical shape',[5] that caused Strauss's initial concern; and Hofmannsthal, seemingly tireless in his search for a solution, recast several scenes in line with his partner's recommendations. He was however prepared to defend a concept which had by now taken firm hold of his imagination, supporting his own confidence with other literary opinions, 'The subject was considered more attractive, more homogeneous and better constructed than *Rosenkavalier*',[6] in his determination to carry the composer along with him. Ultimately the dramatic shape of *Arabella* depended upon Hofmannsthal's positive response to a string of practical proposals put forward by Strauss. Tempered by his own lucid defence of psychological motivation in character and plot, they succeeded in establishing, through the congenial collaborative atmosphere of these years, the most effective formal stage vehicle for the work.

It is hardly surprising that *Arabella*, the embodiment of collaborative hopes and ideals, and with a highly personal literary pedigree, centres, like the earlier 'comedy for music', around the significant and typically Hofmannsthalian concept of 'transformation'. This idea determines the dramatic structure of both works, and is one of the most persistent of that well-defined and related group of ideas which recur as dramatic *Leitmotive* throughout Hofmannsthal's *œuvre*. One of his most fruitful procedural techniques, it is employed to great effect in the prose comedies, particularly in *Der Schwierige*, whose central character has a pre-conceived set of ideas which he is forced, under pressure of changing circumstances, to revise. Of course, inability to adjust to a new situation postulates tragedy – as in *Elektra* – but in such works as *Der Rosenkavalier* and *Ariadne auf Naxos* – as indeed in *Arabella* itself – civilised compromise ultimately restores stability, albeit on a new emotional or conceptual plane. Structurally speaking, this is a process of evolution, instanced in this opera by Arabella's transition from girlhood to womanhood, analogous to the musico-psychological developmental techniques in Strauss's unfailingly symphonic approach.

The idea of transformation which reveals itself as the ultimate spiritual and symbolical goal of so many of Hofmannsthal's works, also manifests itself, during the course of the action, in a more immediate, and theatrically effective manner. Here, catalytic moments arise which are triggered by pivotal, and often spectacular events, of dramatic or psychological significance. Such dramatic turning points are the first encounter between Octavian and Sophie in *Rosenkavalier*, and between Bacchus and Ariadne in *Ariadne auf Naxos*; as well as in Arabella's more subtly conceived successive first-act 'sightings' of Mandryka, which eventually culminate in the meeting and love-declaration of Act 2 and in the betrothal scene of the *finale*. In the case of *Arabella*, such moments, springing naturally from the basic dialogue, are written into the text itself, room being made for musical expression by a controlled heightening of verbal imagery which lends weight, poise, cadence and lyricism to the verse. These episodes, essential to the action, represent a microcosm of that large-scale transformatory principle which determines the nature and symbolism of the drama as a whole. Memorably effected in the two earlier works, they are executed in *Arabella*, in both text and music, with particular delicacy and refinement.

A further important aspect of Hofmannsthal's concept of theatre, related to the idea of transformation, is his obsession with a form of ceremonial whose ritual dignity invests with a deep, almost mystical, significance the course of human existence. *Arabella* was planned around such a series of events. The chief of these, the betrothal scene, although symbolically at the heart of the drama, stands at the very end of the work. This final scene, built in at the instigation of the composer, achieves its climactic effect through those elements of reconciliation and forgiveness so essential to his emotional and dramatic needs. This is markedly different from the shaping of *Der*

Rosenkavalier, where the spectacular Sophie/Octavian meeting, at the high-point of the dramatic arc, has a crucial motivating role in the subsequent action: an equally viable, if more conventional and manageable, architectural solution.

Each phase of the primary action of the work is instigated by the effect upon Arabella of her gradually developing relationship to Mandryka, the stage-by-stage mutual realisation of an apparently unattainable love occurring before the hopeful confirmation of their meeting at the beginning of the second act. This moment of finely judged but, in deference to the *finale*, climactically restrained lyricism, is thus twice anticipated in Act 1 (scenes 3 and 4), and also recollected at the start of the third act (in Arabella's homecoming reflections), before the hard-won spiritual resolution of the ultimate betrothal scene. Psychologically and musically, these anticipatory episodes are significant, giving depth to Arabella's character, and arousing sympathy on her behalf. They constitute a series of emotionally related incidents whose cumulative textual and musical force, ensuring dramatic continuity across the entire three-act span, materially helps to define the emotional boundaries of the work. Indeed, our initial 'bird's-eye' view of the opera, registering the gradual unfolding of Hofmannsthal's psychological and structural design, also recognises that the postponement of the emotional *dénouement* demands the hoarding of the poet's finest effects as well as calling for restraint and anticipatory skill on the part of Strauss: to him it also offers opportunities to exploit an associative key and motivic technique whose coherence is important in delineating the emotional climaxes, and in binding acts and scenes together.

It is characteristic of the Strauss/Hofmannsthal collaboration that close links should be established between literary and musical concepts; nowhere is this 'oneness' of approach so clearly demonstrated as here. Thus, it is not surprising to find the practical Strauss, on receipt of Act 1, urgently requesting details of the subsequent action. 'Above all', he writes, 'I should like to know the further development of the plot and the other two act endings! Couldn't you, in story-telling fashion, dictate the skeleton of the further action, in so far as you have already planned it, and send it to me so that I could gain some slight idea of the whole?'[7] Even at this early stage, efforts to alert Hofmannsthal to the need for 'a string of scenically effective highlights',[8] citing examples such as the Act 1 *levee* scene, the waltz *finale* of Act 2, and the third-act *trio* of *Rosenkavalier*, show the composer's determination to establish a coherent musico-dramatic design.

It was in the careful distribution throughout the opera of these vital moments of emotional and physical contact between Arabella and Mandryka that this purpose was ultimately achieved. Here, Strauss's deployment of key centres deriving psychologically from the allusive character tonalities established in the expository first act also proposes an objective tonal framework which underpins the structure of the drama. Thus, the important Arabella/Mandryka meeting at the beginning of Act 2 revolves specifically around the key of B♭ major; this, clearly representing the emotional transformation taking place at this point, acts in a pivotal tonal capacity, gathering together Arabella's characteristically F major (dominant) hopes from the previous act into a tonic (B♭) resolution, in anticipation of a corresponding cadential strategy which culminates in Mandryka's final 'heroic' E♭ major of the third act.

Ex. 5.1

Act 1   Act 2   Act 3

The *finale* will be examined in more detail later, consisting as it does of an intricate and allusive sequence of keys which define with psychological subtlety the emotional complexities motivating the ultimate union of the lovers. It suffices, for the present, to remark the tonal impetus of the music toward the ultimate structural stability of E♭ major during the course of this act. Here, Mandryka's self-reproach and despair, culminating (Figs. 137–8) on a dominant minor ninth in E♭ major, is magically interrupted by the transition to the C♭ major of the 'staircase' music (a tonal heightening of the earlier ballroom staircase scene), which heralds Arabella's appearance on the hotel landing, and later accompanies her descent to the vestibule. The dramatic suspense created by this harmonic interpolation, the seeds of which are sown at the moment of the lovers' introduction in Act 2 (Ex. 5.2a), is resolved when the interrupted dominant dramatically re-establishes itself at the foot of the stairway (five bars before Fig. 144), its E♭ major destination marking the lovers' reconciliation *en route* for the brief E major (love key) transition – an evocative heightening of the parent tonality and a material lyrical 'gain' for the climax of the work. The restoration of Arabella's F major in the final measures appears, structurally, irrelevant – but, as we shall see, it represents a move of profound psychological significance, emphasising the true nature of her character and contributing importantly to the musical and dramatic shape of the work (Ex. 5.2b).

Ex. 5.2a (Act 2, Fig. 7[6])

Mandryka gazes at Arabella, unable to utter a single word.

Ex. 5.2b

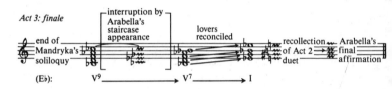

From that vantage point it is possible to assess the expository impact of the first act. The opening scene, dominated by the prophetic utterances of the Fortune-teller, is cleverly designed to introduce the main characters and to predict the course of the action. The situation is tailor-made for Strauss, who at once links Hofmannsthal's textual images decisively to musical *Motiv* and key, so establishing a fund of allusive expressive and illustrative material which is confirmed and developed as the drama unfolds. The first important tonal centre is F major – Arabella's character key – dramatic and musical elements being so designed as to throw her, according to Strauss's professed intention, into the clearest possible relief. Thus at her entrance – the impact of which is heightened by the *angst* of the preceding Zdenka/Matteo scene – for the first time a broader and more settled tonality prevails. This stability of character, mood and key is later emphasised in the Arabella/Zdenka 'Der Richtige' duet, the first recognisable 'set piece' of the act. The positioning of this *scena* (commencing with Arabella's 'Er ist der Richtige nicht für mich' and concluding with the duet), at a crucial phase in the drama, firmly establishes Arabella's needs and affirms her hopes, whilst within a decisive and deliberately conceived

F major key context, explicit references to the first-scene Mandryka *Motiv* ('Der Richtige'), upon which the duet is thematically built, point symbolically towards the E♭ major goal.

A parallel situation occurs several scenes later when Mandryka's characteristically E♭ major arrival, instigating yet another important lyrical climax, establishes the second great tonal pillar of the work. This powerfully extended scene similarly covers a great deal of expository ground as far as Mandryka is concerned, but its structural significance is also apparent. Taken in conjunction with the earlier Arabella passages, her entrance music and the duet, it is clear that the composer has deliberately juxtaposed the two main character-keys of the opera, F major and E♭ major, which will in turn be re-established, though in a different 'psychological' order, in the final act.

Musically, a conclusion might have been reached at this point; but Strauss was aware, as he never tired of reminding Hofmannsthal, that for dramatic reasons the act had to end reflectively. Thus, 'Mein Elemer' confirms the equilibrium that 'Der Richtige' had sought to establish, contributing to the psychological development of the plot, and Arabella's character in particular, as she reaffirms her doubts by reviewing the advantages and rival claims of her lovers. It also presents in symphonic terms – and this act in particular has a specifically symphonic formal unity and design – a summing-up of previously defined leading *Motive* and tonal associations. A sort of mini-recapitulation results as, brushing aside her forebodings, Arabella surrenders herself to the heady A major anticipation of the coming ball.

In relation to the opera as a whole, Act 1, both as music and drama, has an expository function. The purpose of Act 2 is to tighten the dramatic knot and, in Strauss's own words, to provide 'a thrilling transition to the development and denouements of Act 3'.[9] It must be confessed that despite its splendid ballroom setting, an abundance of attractive waltz melodies, and the wild Slavonic excitement of the *finale*, things do not in practice quite measure up to Strauss's persuasive, plausible and apparently coherent design proposals of August 1928. At Hofmannsthal's death the general shape of this act had been decided, but innumerable details remained to be settled. Important and beneficial changes would have been made had the poet lived. This has long been recognised; and attempts have been made over the years to redress the balance of the action – notably by Clemens Krauss, a constant 'improver' of

Strauss's work, who persuaded him to sanction cuts and alterations in Fiakermilli's music, and also hit upon the idea of omitting the choral *finale*, linking Acts 2 and 3 together in an effort to improve the overall dramatic impact.

Ostensibly, in Act 2, the action is divisible into three main sections – the Arabella/Mandryka meeting and courtship culminating in the E major love duet, 'Du wirst mein Gebieter sein'; Arabella's *Abschied* from her earlier lovers; and the mounting orgiastic tension of the Mandryka *finale*. These distinct dramatic phases are complicated by the necessary interweaving of the Matteo/Zdenka sub-plot, effected by means of the *Schlüssel* dialogue (overheard by Mandryka), which instigates the final climactic scene. Furthermore, the need to provide an element of dramatic contrast between the lyrical opening 'courtship scene' and the tender *Abschied* cameos at the act's centre brought about the first excursion into the ballroom with its tuneful waltzes, champagne, flowers and that epitomic *Kutscher* mascot, Fiakermilli.

If this second act is less effective than the first, wherein does its failure lie? One potential source of trouble was to some extent averted when Strauss hit upon the idea – already used successfully in *Rosenkavalier* – of using a continuous waltz sequence to underpin the episodic nature of the central and final sections, where all the comings and goings, assignations, flirtations and conspiracies threaten to disrupt the natural flow of the action. This strategy provided an appropriate unifying framework upon which the events of the drama could unfold. Nevertheless these scenes still require careful handling in performance, and this is particularly true of the *finale*, which has been the real sticking point for most critics, and to which drastic remedies have sometimes been applied. The main problem – an inherent, overall, proportional imbalance – stems from the uncertain dramatic construction of the act. It is apparent in performance, that in weight, significance, scope and musical coherence, the Mandryka/Fiakermilli *finale* does not adequately match the sustained and expressive opening Arabella/Mandryka scene. The resultant structural and emotional imbalance between these two important flanking sections of the work induces a sense of anticlimax towards the act's conclusion which even Strauss' technique and experience was unable entirely to eradicate. At this point the tragedy of Hofmannsthal's death took its toll. It is clear that so fundamental a problem could not be resolved – even if its nature had been recognised – without major textual revision, and this Strauss refused to consider. There was no alternative but to impose an arbitrary solution: a deliberate adoption of the strategy employed in the second act of *Die Fledermaus*, a solution which – despite the orchestral brilliance and savagery of Mandryka's wild climactic 'folk-song' ballad – predictably misses the infectious excitement of that earlier, and as far as the central act of *Arabella* was concerned, crucially 'generic' masterwork.

Arabella, one remembers, was originally conceived as a combination of two distinct dramatic ideas of which, in the event, *Lucidor* played by far the more important part. The preferential development of the Arabella role at the expense of the Lucidor/Lucile element naturally caused the collaborators some headaches; but while in general terms the structure of the opera depends upon the progress of the relationship between Arabella and Mandryka, one also recognises the importance of the Zdenka/Matteo sub-plot, whose deliberately low-key exploitation in Act 1 defines a tumultuous romantic liaison of quite a different order. With the delivery of Arabella's bedroom key to Matteo in Act 2, this secondary idea not only arrives at a crucial turning point in its own development but also for the first time impinges significantly upon the main argument, administering a dramatic shot in the arm which generates the tension needed to motivate the events of the subsequent act.

It makes excellent musical and dramatic sense that the keys which define Zdenka and Matteo (Bb major, G major and E minor) are, throughout the opera, less clear-cut in application than those relating to the other main protagonists: and so conflicts of tonal precedence which might blur the outlines of the primary action are avoided. By the same token a less securely anchored tonal basis, with the potential for lightning alternations of key, serves as a vivid illustration of the emotional insecurity, impulsiveness, frustration and immaturity of these youthful, impassioned figures and, grants a certain modulatory freedom useful in propelling the music toward its short-term expressive and architectural goals. In the wider tonal sense, the opening scene progresses from the structural but equally emotive Bb major of the Arabella/Mandryka meeting, to the E major love duet (another great lyric landmark of the score), employing, en route, the most detailed psychological development of theme and key. Similarly, the equally allusive and nostalgic lyrical *Adieux* of the central episodes reach a moving B major climax in the tenderness of Arabella's farewell to Lamoral. Now, Zdenka's confrontation of Matteo leads to a gradual intensification of Mandryka's jealousy, culminating in his daemonic Croatian ballad – a spiteful G minor parody of the earlier love duet of this act. This, fuelled by his drunken flirtation with Milli, gathers fresh impetus as the composer, abandoning psychological associative devices, switches to 'situation' keys or illustrative effects, or adopts less personal and more traditional tonal symbolism such as the defiantly festive and brilliant D major of the concluding ensemble.

Something has been said in the foregoing paragraphs about musical and dramatic weaknesses in Act 2. Few indeed are the operas that could bear detailed investigation and escape unscathed. The recognition of specific problems enables one to place them within a wider perspective and to relate them to the work as a whole. *Arabella* may be less than perfect, and for this Hofmannsthal's death is undoubtedly to blame, but it had the potential to become the masterpiece of the Strauss/Hofmannsthal collaboration. It is our good fortune that this potential shines through so consistently, not only in the unsurpassable first act but significantly and consistently, for all the hesitations and *longueurs*, over its entire span – the music, catching inspiration from the text, rarely failing at the crucial moments to soar to unforgettable heights.

It is in this spirit that one should regard the third act, whose deeply humane voice, emerging so inevitably from the trauma of events, makes it a moving operatic experience. Its four substantial scenes are constituted as follows:

(a)   The *Prelude*, Arabella's entrance, her *air* and altercation with Matteo up to. . .

(b)   The arrival of Mandryka and the Waldners whose accusations of infidelity are interrupted by the prospective duel and. . .

(c)   A distraught Zdenka whose appearance, culminating in her betrothal to Matteo, begins the general process of reconciliation which is. . .

(d)   Completed by the 'staircase' scene, the enactment of the village betrothal 'rite' and the lovers' final affirmations.

The *Prelude*, as well as being of the highest dramatic significance, also proves to be an essential structural feature of the whole first scene. Vividly depicting the amorous encounter between Matteo and the 'supposed' Arabella, its tonal and motivic elements eventually return, almost in a recapitulatory sense, to mark the climax and to complete the first phase of the musical design. Commencing in G major with the folksong-like simplicity of Arabella's *Lied*, the scene demonstrates, in Matteo's triumphant, puzzled and, for Arabella, embarrassing declarations, an increasingly impassioned melodic utterance which accurately reflects the gradual poetic heightening of the words. Although frequently interrupted by Arabella's exasperated protestations, this lyrical framework supplies an overall expressive continuity which culminates in the emphatic and unambiguous restatement of the introductory E major and its attendant thematic material.

While (a) develops an essential lyricism out of its initially 'conversational' nature, its successor, (b), is deliberately designed to heighten the dramatic tension, reverting to a pronounced, directly contrasted, swiftly-moving declamatory style. At the Waldners' entrance (F minor), a modulatory key sequence is initiated which, progressing unremittingly towards Zdenka's revelatory G major, establishes the climax by means of increasing harmonic complexity and additional weight of scoring. To Arabella alone is granted consistent tonal stability – an effective exercise in character delineation which succeeds in throwing her into sharp relief against a background of emotional confusion; so emphasising her unassailable integrity in the face of unfounded accusations and suspicions. Not only is Arabella tonally so defined; she is also distinguished by a noble simplicity of vocal line, and warm, predominantly string, accompanying textures denied to other characters. These features, which are from now on progressively expanded, anticipate the increasingly lyrical outpourings of (c), and presage the reconciliatory melodic distillations of the Arabella/Mandryka *finale*.

These two final scenes are linked together, not least by this generous melodic flow which reaches its initial climax as Mandryka intercedes on behalf of Zdenka and her lover. Their ecstasy, having passed through the emotionally rich Straussian keys D♭, G♭, B and F♯ major, is interrupted, as Arabella's tentative forgiveness of Mandryka restores the 'flat' tonalities, bringing the music to a dramatic halt on the dominant seventh chord of B♭ major. Now follows Mandryka's plea to Waldner, 'Brautwerbung kommt!' (D major), after which the delayed dominant resolution on to B♭ major initiates the *finale*.

As for this miraculous final scene, little needs to be said. Such effects were, as Strauss knew, always his strong suit. The apparently inexhaustible lyrical flow of the music reflects, with the most intimate nuance, the magic and simplicity of Hofmannsthal's concept. A supreme economy of texture employs *Motiv* and key so as to make every point tell – an overwhelming musical and theatrical climax, whose powerful visual impact has a decisive dramatic effect. Form, expression and means combine as the music sets out to resolve, inevitable though such a resolution might be, an as yet fluid emotional

situation. The element of suspense, a further tribute to Hofmannsthal's genius, doubtless has its part to play before the smashing of the
glass by Mandryka signifies that the transformation is complete –
Arabella's girlhood is truly over, and her final F major affirmation –
'Nimm mich wie ich bin!' – symbolises her embracing of her destiny.

6 Analysis: technique and expression

Not only is the structural importance of tonality paramount in *Arabella*; key also plays a concurrent expressive role in the opera, interpreting the nature of those emotional climaxes which determine the overall shape of the drama. All Strauss's music is diatonically based: his operatic 'roots' reach back to Wagner, for whose musical and literary achievements he showed life-long reverence and admiration. In common with other late nineteenth-century composers it was directly from this source that Strauss inherited a key-association and leitmotivic technique which Wagner had himself developed from an earlier classical tradition. Drawing inevitably upon such 'received' associative patterns, Strauss evolved personal tonal procedures to suit his own individual needs as well as to express the form and dramatic content of his subjects.

Each of the Strauss operas inhabits its own tonal world, the nature of which is determined by a distinctive 'localised' set of character- and situation-keys. These are inevitably grouped around a further series of 'core' tonalities, reflecting a range of more universal emotional and spiritual attributes, which remain constant and valid for his entire *œuvre*. This, combined with an explicit 'leitmotivic' technique, offers an highly-developed interpretative procedure capable of reflecting the course of the drama with astonishing accuracy. Strauss's aims were threefold: simultaneously to reinforce and interpret the psychological detail of the action; to define the emotional shape; and to determine the formal musical structure of the work.

Wagner's perception of the function of drama in relation to music, which resulted in the preparation of his own texts, exerted a profound influence upon his contemporaries. His achievement in *The Ring* and in *Tristan* brought increasing demands for libretti of a distinctive literary quality in the middle to late nineteenth century. It was not however until the Strauss/Hofmannsthal collaboration of 1906 that a composer of outstanding genius formed a stable working

75

relationship with a writer of equal importance. 'I know that for many generations past no distinguished poet of the rank with which I may credit myself amongst the living, has dedicated himself willingly and devotedly to the task of working for a musician',[1] Hofmannsthal wrote in 1911; and both partners were conscious of 'the prospect of beauty which will be called into being by a union of our two arts. . .a perfect harmony of seeing and hearing'.[2]

Undoubtedly, Strauss sensed something of that mystic element in his partner's work which explores 'a world of spirituality higher and deeper and freer than words allow for';[3] but the true strength of their association lies in Hofmannsthal's realisation of a poetic concept which is not inherently self-sufficient but relies for its total effect upon a combination of art-forms of which the most significant is music. 'Hofmannsthal's opera text is unique because it comes so near to poetic independence and yet remains conscious that music will enhance it',[4] comments Ronald Peacock, and it was precisely the nature of this 'extraordinarily fine artistic calculation', resulting in an expressive idiomatic textual flexibility, that enabled Strauss to develop the conversational or *parlando* style of writing of which *Arabella* also provides so apt a demonstration. It is not difficult to understand how Strauss, after working with Hofmannsthal, pleaded with subsequent librettists such as Gregor and Krauss for 'Prose not poetry!' – an anguished counterpoint which runs consistently through his later creative years.

Hofmannsthal's experience as a dramatist perfectly fitted him to fulfil Strauss's needs in collaborative theatre. The first scene of *Arabella*, for instance, provides an excellent example of swiftly-moving dialogue, skilfully designed to initiate the action and to introduce the most important characters. Its prediction of future events also provides opportunity for the composer to 'set up' many of the essential tonal and motivic associations of the work. Nowhere else is Hofmannsthal's instinctive understanding of the expositional requirements of the leitmotivic opera so aptly or so naturally displayed. Indeed, the oracular nature of the dialogue between the anxious mother and the clairvoyant enables the composer to introduce at least fifteen separate melodic *Motive* and to define some of the more important tonal centres – all of which will be expanded and developed during the course of the action. The passage is no less skilfully orchestrated; individual, delicately balanced instrumental timbres comprising various groupings of strings, woodwind or brass highlight a notable restraint in scoring – thus ensuring maximum audibility of voice and text. The instrumental deployment inevitably also serves an expressive purpose – as for instance in the evocation of Mandryka's forest fastnesses (*pianissimo* trombones) or the characteristic horn treatment of the 'Der Richtige' (the 'right man') theme.

Hofmannsthal's achievement is at its most effective in passages where the developing dramatic situation inspires him to cross the boundary between poetry and prose. These moments are important turning-points in the course of the action. Here, an emotional 'contouring' of the dialogue is effected by a fleeting, barely perceptible transition to verbal lyricism which always secures a correspondingly meaningful response from the composer. Fine control over sonority and rhythmic flow enables the poet to hover delicately on the borderline between the inspirational and the mundane, the instantaneous switch from one emotional level or mood to another reflecting the passions and capturing the essence of those longings that spring momentarily from beneath the surface of the verbal argument. Moments such as these are seldom prolonged in Hofmannsthal, save where a deliberate emotional climax in the shape of an *arioso*, *aria* or ensemble is intended, as in the final scene of the first act. For the most part the musician has free rein to expand the emotive idea, to exploit that expressive lyricism which emerges from the recitative-like context without the strait-jacket of a heavy, rhythmically syllabic or restrictively rhyming text to hinder him – by such means, indeed, Hofmannsthal 'achieves the right density and the proper rhythmic elasticity for language that is to be supported by music; an equilibrium of melody, movement, clarity, sentiment and image that is perfectly appropriate'.[5]

Two passages demonstrate this technique of verbal heightening. The first, taken from Act 1, scene 4 (89^7–92^7), occurs after Elemer's exit and precedes the entrance of the Waldners prior to the big Mandryka scene. The second, the 'Mein Elemer' *finale* (157^{10}–162^3), is representative of the more sustained emotional climax which, despite its 'dialogue' roots, shows how the composer creates from motivic elements an expressive, continuous lyricism of singular associative and dramatic significance.

In order to support this discussion it is necessary to be more specific about the function of key and *Motiv*. A number of significant key centres have been identified during the course of this study; the whole tonal spectrum can best be demonstrated in diagrammatic form (see below). The circle of tonalities divides naturally across a north/south axis. The southern arc, A–C–Eb, appar-

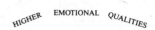

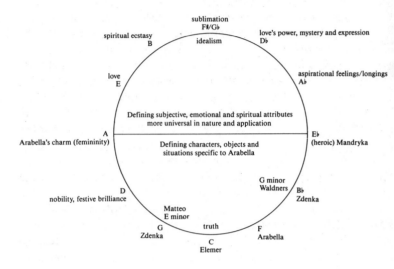

ently represents keys which define characters, objects and situations specific to this particular work, whilst the northern, A–F♯–E♭, identifies tonalities which depict subjective feeling, or emotional and spiritual attributes of a more universal nature. This apparently arbitrary ordering of the tonal scheme is far from unusual in Strauss; indeed, it is no exaggeration to say that all his operas demonstrate similar associative tonal organisation, indicating the craftsmanship and planning which underlie their composition. Thus, whilst the keys plotted along the southern arc apply solely to *Arabella*, those defined by the northern describe states of being such as love (E major) or inspirational power (D♭ major) – attributes sometimes hard to define but whose allusory significance remained constant in Strauss's music throughout his career. Minor keys figure less importantly as a general rule – depicting for the most part negative aspects of qualities represented by principal major tonalities: thus, E♭ minor in Act 3, scenes 2 (53³) and 3 (74) represents Arabella's disappointment at Mandryka's (E♭ major) unfounded suspicions; whilst in the scene discussed below, A♭ minor, negating the ecstatic D♭ major aspirations of A♭ major, is suggestive of failure to achieve the longed-for 'love' ideal. Similarly, we find the Waldners' somewhat seedy social status given a G minor flavour, although E minor is exceptionally also associated with Matteo, so establishing a tonal link (through the relative minor association), with Zdenka's G major, a device which binds these two characters together emotionally long before the revelation of their love in the final act of the opera.

The *Motive* of the opera also exist on different interpretative levels – some being merely of passing significance such as the *Lohengrin* (24[14]) and 'silver rose' (39[1]; from *Der Rosenkavalier*) quotations in Act 1, whereas others depict individual moods or aspects of character. Some characters, such as Elemer and Matteo, who are secondary in importance, are represented by a definitive and limited number of musical ideas which summarise their whole personality and presence. Others – Arabella, Mandryka and Zdenka – who play a central part in the drama, each have a complex group of associative melodies descriptive of differing aspects of their natures, aspirations and attitudes. It is hardly possible to provide a full lexicon of such *Motive*, nor is it necessary. Those introduced here for the first time will be identified on the spot, while for others, the reader is referred back to Chapter 2, where the dominant melodic ideas have been stated within the context of the action. The aim is to gain some insight into the manner in which Strauss employs his tonal and thematic material, to interpret the drama and to provide a blueprint that can be applied to other passages in the work. Ex. 6.1, consisting of twenty-nine bars, gives a typical example of this transition into and out of heightened dialogue and musically lyrical style.

Ex. 6.1 (Act 1, Fig. 89[8])

Ex. 6.1 (*cont.*)

Ex. 6.1 (*cont.*)

Elemer? *Ar*: Ja, ja. Geh' und zieh' dich an.   Du fährst mit uns.   Ich will's.   *Zd*: Pst, die Mama.

The restless figure (a) of bars 1–4 depicts the pawing of Elemer's horses as they await Arabella in the street outside the hotel. As she gazes from the window, her thoughts, the C major dominant tells us, are of Elemer, and the impending excursion to the Prater. The unexpected resolution of this dominant to Ab minor (1*) registers her shock at the sight of Mandryka in the street below. The suspense is heightened by tremolo strings, while ascending semiquaver clarinet figures (b) – the latter already established as descriptive of Arabella's high-spirited charm – also suggest her agitation at the unexpected reappearance of her handsome stranger. All these musical elements are accompanied by a rhythmic, scalic bass clarinet passage (c) derived from the Mandryka theme (Ex. 2.7), which also happens to be closely related to the 'longing' *Motiv* shortly to make its appearance as (f) in bars 8–9. As Arabella establishes beyond doubt the identity of the stranger (2*), the characteristic Mandryka theme rings out uncompromisingly in Eb major, on horns and strings (d). The succeeding vocal recitative, picking out the 'right man' theme (e), memorably utilised in the Arabella/Zdenka duet, now intensifies her hopes, transforming the original Ab minor of bar 4 into the major (3*) preparatory to the introduction of the 'longing' *Motiv* (f), which, stated in the lower strings, registers Arabella's mounting excitement. Now passing swiftly through A major (4*), the passage culminates in a triumphant assertion of the chord of Eb major, the Mandryka key (5*).

Up to this point the pace of recitative, supported by deftly expressive instrumentation, has mirrored the objective nature of Arabella's commentary. Now, summoning Zdenka to her side, she hazards an interpretation of the stranger's actions as he gazes at the hotel facade. 'He's trying to work out where my windows are', she informs Zdenka, and the note patterns once again outline the 'longing' *Motiv* (f'). This time, the expansion of the initial intervals, foreshadowing the opening of the staircase theme (Ex. 2.8), reminds us that Strauss's deliberately 'symphonic' approach to his material also uncovers unsuspected 'psychological' relationships between representative personalities and themes in the work.

Now, Hofmannsthal's dialogue takes on, transitorily, a more lyrical vein. Arabella's 'Schau seine Augen an, was das für große ernste Augen sind' ('Just look at his eyes – Oh what great serious eyes he has'), springing, as it does, from the depths of her being, demands musical emphasis to match the poetic mood. Strauss's response broadens the rhythmic flow, an anticipatory, syncopated figure (g) (of later importance), measuring out a heady crotchet sequence as prevailing E♭ major (Mandryka) melts into the passionate tenderness of E major (6*). Two trumpets join the strings in their accompaniment of these emotive descending phrases (reminiscent of the central stanza of the Arabella/Zdenka duet) whilst the 'longing' idea repeated five times in diminution on the violas (f″) indicates the emotional turmoil raging in Arabella's breast.

At the conclusion of this glorious passage, Mandryka's theme (d) reappears softly in the strings, nostalgically tinged with E major harmonies (Arabella's wistful love-sick musings), before the magic dissolves into prosaic A minor at Zdenka's decidedly waspish rejoinder (7*). The final echo of this ascending string figure (h) is compounded of the second strain of the Mandryka theme and the final phase of (f), which, now shorn of its rhythmic characteristics, stretches the 'longing' sequence of rising intervals through a conflict of harmonically inspired emotions as Arabella acknowledges the futility of her hopes (8*). As this brief evocative interlude nears its end, A♭ major returns with a plaintive echo of the 'right man' *Motiv* (e), which, alternating uncertainly between that key and E minor (love rejection), combines an inversion of the theme of 'longing' (chromatically extended on the bass clarinet) (f″) with the wistful tones of (d) sounded in the flute and muted first violins, as Mandryka, to Arabella's intense disappointment, passes by in the street outside. The vocal line now reverts to a *parlando* manner although the lyrically heightened mood lingers in the orchestra. Alternations of A♭ major, E minor and E♭ major tell their own tale until a tentative C minor reasserts Elemer's rights to Arabella's company (9*) if also her reluctance to change her dream prospects for reality. The final bar (dominant seventh in G minor) prepares for the Waldners' arrival and the onset of the big Mandryka scene.

Passages of this nature abound in *Arabella*, although not all involve such concentrated manipulation of materials as that above.

Many are the moments where music and action, as in the opening scene, must move at a pace which precludes reflection in order to forward the dramatic argument. As one would expect, those flights of lyricism which mark the intermediary affective climaxes of the work become more expansive and more insistent at the approach of larger-scale emotional statements, which, even in *durchkomponiert* opera, equate with the older set forms of aria, duet and multiple ensemble. Such 'preparations', ostensibly overflowing into 'arioso', precede all the 'set pieces' in *Arabella*, although Strauss, having ultimately rejected plans for a quartet in Act 1, depends solely upon duet and solo scene for the 'set pieces' of the score.

The lyrical outpouring which concludes the first act constitutes just such a highlight. 'Mein Elemer' is, indeed, less an aria than a complex dramatic *scena*; an 'in depth' study of Arabella at a turning point in her emotional career. Here, we have a glimpse of the real woman faced with decisions which will determine her own destiny and that of her family. The progress of her moods, through doubt, rejection, tenderness, hope and despair to anticipatory delight in the evening's ball, offers musical summary as well as psychological development, gathering together the threads of the action in an almost recapitulatory manner. The effectiveness of the on-stage situation is enhanced by the audience's awareness of Mandryka's enrolment as a suitor – a dramatic development as yet unknown to Arabella herself.

'Mein Elemer!' takes its cue from a brief recitative in which Arabella chides her sister for taking so long to dress for the excursion to the Prater. 'Those horses and your Elemer!' retorts Zdenka, as she flounces indignantly out of the room; the lively rhythmic inflection of her 'Dein Elemer!' (a jagged, descending minor-seventh interval) sparking off an orchestral lyricism which from this point onward plays a significant interpretative role. The instruments now weave together melodic strands derived from previously heard *Motive*, to provide a continuous, colourful and expressive commentary upon the physical and psychological action. The orchestral argument is, at first, paramount – intermittent vocal phrases tending either to confirm instrumental conclusions and to add immediacy to instrumental climaxes, or to initiate new ideas which serve to redirect the course and nature of the prevailing argument. Ultimately, however, the voice assumes its inevitable and natural lyric role, in long anticipated, increasingly expressive melodic statements which culminate in waltz-like exhilaration at the prospect of the ball.

The resultant expressive interchange between voice and orchestra, won from a concentrated manipulation of *Motive* and of keys, shows itself in a 'narrative' lyric technique which springs naturally out of, and contributes importantly to, the dramatic situation. The effectiveness, indeed the necessity, for 'Mein Elemer' at the end of Act 1 was never in doubt, so far as Strauss was concerned; it gave him an important opportunity to spread himself lyrically, as well as providing an effective curtain for the first act. Essentially, the musical argument is focussed on a motivically highly organised, and primarily instrumental, melodising, articulate support being provided by a variety of countersubjects (Ex. 6.2).

Ex. 6.2 (Act 1, Fig. 157[10])

The passage is typical of the allusive polyphonic complexity and expressive power at the composer's command. The dissonant wood-wind harmonies of 'Dein Elemer' (x), echoing Zdenka's unaccompanied, somewhat petulant riposte, are starkly dramatic, suggesting the indecision with which her sister is faced. The essential melodic line is, throughout, entrusted to the solo viola, whose reflective tones are appropriate to Arabella's sombre musings (f). This continuous melodic presence may be seen as typical of Strauss's large-scale lyricism. It proposes specific key and instrumental 'mood' colourings, while also, by means of its motivic construction, interpreting and initiating the psycho-dramatic argument. Such melodising attains even greater allusive subtlety and significance through the polyphonic interweaving of the subsidiary motivic voices which accompany it. An idea formerly representative of her high-spirited femininity, (i), straightway plunges the music into an emotionally highly charged C♯ minor whose enharmonic D♭ minor aspect mirrors the doubts which torment her soul. Her preoccupation is confirmed by a reflective variant of a further Arabella idea (j) (lower strings and woodwind) which reappears, encompassing the femininity *Motiv* (i), against the Elemer theme (k) (first horn) – discouragingly answered (for Elemer) by the 'right man' idea (e) (oboes and clarinets), in the C♯ minor key. These elements, in combination with (j), (i), and (f), culminate in a tonally heightened repetition of the agonised 'Mein Elemer' figure (x), which introduces the voice for the first time.

This allusive contrapuntal brew is kept simmering for the next seventeen bars, the solo viola and the oboe, here as elsewhere in the opera individually expressive of Arabella's character, mirroring her thoughts, which lead via rhetorical statements of doubt (x) and the sequentially insistent Elemer *Motiv* (k) to a discreet affirmation of his characteristic C major fanfare on muted trumpets and horns. Arabella's confusion, still firmly grounded in C major, is demonstrated by a canonic insistence on (x), 'He mine! – I his!. . .why do I feel such dread?', which, ultimately returning to negate the 'celli's fleeting suggestion of the 'right man' theme (Ex. 6.3), initiates a new direction in the musical and dramatic argument.

Ex. 6.3 (Act 1, Fig. 160[6])

Ex. 6.3 (*cont.*)

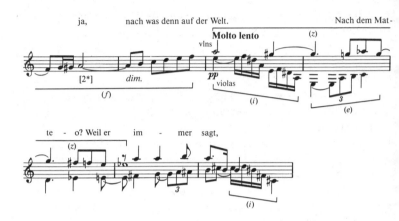

At this point, Arabella's emotional struggle (viola (f)) intensifies. 'What in the whole world can assuage this inexpressible yearning?' she sings, the emphasis now, for the first time, securely upon the voice which floats clear above a rising tide of instrumental sound (2*). A characteristically feminine gesture (i) breaks into her A minor hesitations, before the Matteo/Zdenka passion *Motiv* (z) (Ex. 2.1c) prepares the introduction of Matteo's characteristic E minor, expressing *en route* a humane B♭ tenderness for his childlike devotion and boyish commitment. Her dismissive 'But Matteo doesn't arouse my deepest feelings' confirms his rejection, while at the same time a doleful version of the 'right man' theme ('celli) indicates that her thoughts are moving in a new direction. This reappearance of (e) represents a lyrical intensification which gathers momentum after the very significant transition to D♭ major (Ex. 6.4, (3*) below), the first extended melodic climax of the scene, as Arabella recollects the mysterious stranger who, with his 'great eyes and serious mien', represents the goal of her emotional quest.

The move to D♭ major is of particular interest, since Arabella's two previous and preparatory Mandryka street 'sightings' (full score, p. 68 and p. 80 above) are each centred upon the related key of A♭ major. Just as we have defined in Chapter 5 a series of dominant-tonic relationships whose allusive and structural significance straddles the score from scene to scene and from act to act, so here this

D♭ major 'arrival' signifies a preliminary stage in the progress towards 'emotional' fulfilment; it represents a further example of Strauss's ability, by virtue of interlocking tonal devices, this time within the course of an act, to achieve meaningful and psychologically valid structural procedures. A complex and evocative orchestral texture marks the significance of this climactic passage, creating a delicate web of sound by its employment of thirteen-part string divisions, including three solo violins, and three solo violas, the whole discreetly supported by woodwind and horns.

Ex. 6.4 (Act 1, Fig. 163⁴)

Naturally, the expression of such intimate yearnings demands, above all, vocal sovereignty, and Strauss achieves this clear dramatic requirement by reverting to a relatively homophonic accompaniment during the course of the passage. Drawn from elements of the 'right man' duet, Arabella's breathtakingly melodic 'I would have liked to see my stranger once again! I wish I could have heard his voice just once' is inevitably but discreetly accompanied by (f) ('celli and bassoon), whilst the 'confident' four-note 'Der Richtige' *Motiv* (e) in due course dominates a passionate emotional climax (4*), before the dream moment fades toward an indecisive F♯ minor tonality. The narrative melody now continues for another twenty-four bars in the form of an oboe and viola (now full section) duet, to culminate in an emphatic statement of the Zdenka/Matteo 'passion' theme (Ex. 2.1c) as tremolo strings anticipate the fateful return of the 'Mein Elemer' figure (for the last time).

This marks the beginning of the second part of the *scena*, which like its successor is divisible into two subsidiary sections, the first rhetorical and recitative-like, the second more lyrical and therefore climactic in effect. This time, after the brief recapitulatory 'Verheirat't mit dem Elemer?', a passage directly comparable with the opening (return of C♯ minor), the solo viola shares its expressive role with the first violins and the 'celli, amalgamating elements of (x), (j), (f) and (i), and subsequently combining with the voice itself as Arabella reflects on her stranger's uncanny power over her. Once again the music progresses to a lyrical climax, the *'Der Richtige' Motiv*, serenely floated on clarinets and strings, intertwining with the voice ((e) and (f), with inversion and extensions of the latter), to suffer tonal retrenchment to A♭ major as Arabella resigns herself to her destiny. Her dream is over; certainly her stranger is a married man; how unlikely it is that she will even see him again (Ex. 6.5).

Such evocative treatment of vocal and instrumental lines and such sustained melodising are typical of Strauss's later work. The aura of divided strings combines with the waltz-like flute roulades (f^1) as Arabella wistfully concludes her lingering A♭ major cadence. Gently, almost tenderly, the orchestra side-steps enharmonically into C♯ minor, preparatory to bright A major, heartening her with intimations of the coming ball, and shyly embarking upon the slow waltz that characterises the remainder of the scene (5*). At first the lilting rhythm indulges Arabella's sadness, toying with the 'charm' (j), 'right man' (e) and 'longing' (f) *Motive*. Eventually, however, the mood brightens and her irrepressible high spirits reassert themselves

Ex. 6.5 (Act 1, Fig. 169)

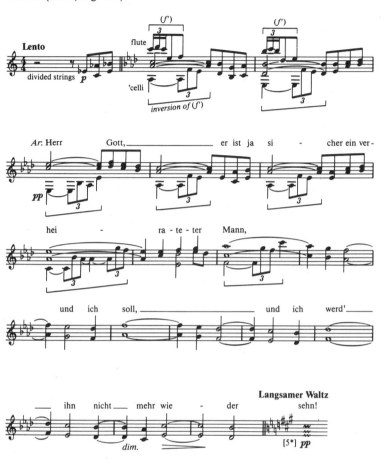

in ecstatic anticipation of the *Faschingsball* of which she is to be queen. Zdenka's arrival, interrupting her exultation, is reflected in a languorous string version of Ex. 2.1c which, uniting with elements of (f), sparks off an exciting orchestral coda, the orchestra emphatically insisting upon the impetuous Elemer *Motiv* (k) to conclude the act as the sisters join him in his carriage in the not entirely unexpected key of C major.

This remarkable psychological portrait achieves structural coherence through the composer's ability to interpret the logical progression of Arabella's musings in terms of an inspired, motivically articulate, melodic commentary whose characteristic viola presence also proposes a symphonic thread which unifies the whole. The inevitable movement of each section towards lyricism is inherent in Hofmannsthal's text, as, indeed, are the final ballroom anticipations which gave Strauss the opportunity to crown the act with colour, rhythm, excitement and youthful optimism. Its composition must have been a moving experience for him, as he set lines written only two days before Hofmannsthal's tragic death.

As a combination of art, inspiration and craftsmanship, this *finale* is unsurpassed, demonstrating a new flexibility of approach which was to bear fruit later in the first Maria scene of *Friedenstag*, and in the *Capriccio finale*. It was Strauss who commented in later years to Stefan Zweig that he had succeeded in finding a path around the Wagner mountain. In this first act finale, as elsewhere in *Arabella*, we might find evidence of the truth of this statement. Strauss's highly chromatic melodic idiom, supported by a relatively uncluttered and predominantly diatonic harmonic framework, directly contrasts with the more purposeful harmonic progress of the Wagnerian manner. It is this very harmonic 'space' created around his ideas which gives Strauss the opportunity for that polyphonic and melodic expressivity so clearly demonstrated in the 'Mein Elemer' passage. Most importantly, as a *dénouement*, it emerges naturally as a truthful response to a developing and credible dramatic situation, thus reflecting Hofmannsthal's ideal concept of theatre. Strauss's genius enabled him to produce here, not for the first time, through the effect of solo voice and orchestra, a powerful human climax, in defiance of the formula of duet or multiple ensemble so essential to his Italian contemporaries. It is the psychological truths so intimately expressed in the text and so magically distilled through the music that allow the realisation of the phenomenon. Such high artistic rationality shows the Strauss/Hofmannsthal collaboration in its truest and best light.

7 The Act 3 sketchbook

Strauss naturally spent time over the assimilation of a new libretto before embarking on its composition. So far as his work with Hofmannsthal was concerned, the shaping of the text was to some extent a joint exercise, and by the time the finished drafts had materialised, many of the musical ideas had already become clear in his mind. During this period and subsequently, the poet's manuscript was invariably very carefully annotated by the composer, important key centres, *Motive* and procedural comments being jotted down in the margins as his creative instincts were quickened by dramatic situation and verbal imagery. It was clearly during these precompositional stages that the overall associative tonal picture and the melodic and harmonic character of the piece took shape in his mind.

Generally speaking, Strauss was quick to seize upon any illustrative aspects of a text which could contribute towards the individual colour and atmosphere of a work. His facility in this respect is well known, and there are numerous instances in *Arabella* – the champing of Elemer's horses or Mandryka's description of his encounter with a bear – where he was able to indulge this gift for musical mimicry. Self-quotation and borrowings from other composers are also used, as in Act 1 of the opera, where the silver rose *Motiv* from *Der Rosenkavalier* is used to depict Arabella's bouquet. Earlier, in scene 1, material from Wagner's *Lohengrin* puts in a brief appearance, a pedagogical and topical allusion provoked by Matteo's jealous concern over Arabella's evening theatrical excursions.[1]

One is also keenly aware in this work of the Croatian folk-song element which Strauss worked into the score in response to Hofmannsthal's inclusion of Mandryka in the plot. These 'ethnic' ideas, particularly noticeable in the wild Act 2 *finale*, are also evidenced in the two great duets[2], the basic material of which had been culled from an authentic collection of Slavonic *Lieder* which Strauss had been exploring as early as 1927. While this folk-song influence is most clearly observed in the examples cited above, its character 'colours' the entire score, adding a subtle cohesion to the work's musical structure. One notices, in the third act particularly, a deliberate attempt to employ such ideas in a recapitulatory manner through direct quotation: in Arabella's opening song, for instance, or in the glowing reminiscence of the Slavonic betrothal custom of the final scenes. That so many of the important *Motive* of the opera are derived from these central folk-song ideas invests the work with a unique coherence and demonstrates the remarkable refinement of Strauss's symphonic procedures.

Throughout his composing life, Strauss carried pocket notebooks into which he transcribed musical ideas as they occurred to him. Of these volumes, 135 have been preserved in the Garmisch archive – all of which, transferred to microfilm, are now available for study in the Bayerische Staatsbibliothek in Munich. Other such sketchbooks exist in libraries and private collections throughout Europe, their wide dissemination resulting from the composer's habit of presenting them to colleagues in recognition of musical services or as a mark of friendship. Clearly, once a work was completed, such jottings no longer had any intrinsic value in his eyes. Doubtless many more of these books will come to light – they constitute a mine of information on Strauss's compositional and organisational procedures and afford a 'behind the scenes' glimpse of the practical and technical expertise employed to bring the creative impulse into focus.

The Act 3 sketchbook that Strauss donated to Hermann Kutzschbach in 1935 to mark the fortieth Dresden performance of *Arabella* is in the *Musiksammlung* of the Österreichische Nationalbibliothek in Vienna. Its contents comprise most of the material for the final two scenes of the opera, commencing at Zdenka's entry (Fig. 91, v.s. p. 317), as far the orchestral flourish (Fig. 144, v.s. p. 357) which concludes the 'interruption' of Arabella's staircase descent. This comes to rest on the Bb major chord prior to the Eb major resolution which depicts the reconciliation of the lovers. Only the final 143 bars remain to be continued in a further volume.

A first reaction on examination of these drafts is incredulity at the fluency and detail they display when compared with the completed score. While at times the melodic working is supported merely by outline harmonies, frequently every facet of the harmony and contrapuntal texture of the final version is noted. It is hard to believe that other, preliminary, sketches did not precede these drafts – although,

since the third act of an opera inevitably finds the con
stocked' with materials, *Motive*, ideas and structural ʏ
should not be surprised that the melodic gifts and manipulɑ
of the symphonic composer could operate to such apparent
taneous effect. A typical example of this fluency and atten
detail is demonstrated in Plate 9a (p. 9 of the sketchbook, Fiɡ
v.s. pp. 323–5). Here, at the sound of Zdenka's voice Matteo pour
his soul in a brief lyrical effusion, 'Welch süße Stimme ruft mich ɛ
(Whose is the sweet voice that calls to me?). Although details of t
bass figurations were to be added later, the interrogative 'stridinɡ
Matteo *Motiv* (see Ex. 2.3) is plainly seen in the tenor at bars 3 and ᔰ
as well as its syncopated continuation in the inner parts, which are
faithfully reproduced in the final score. The change from triple to
quadruple time is also clearly marked at the double bar-line and the
entire passage shows the composer in full lyrical flow, displaying
complete confidence in the control and integration of motivic
material which is, appropriately enough, dominated by the Zdenka/
Matteo 'passion' figure (see Ex. 2.1c).

It was from workings such as these that the vocal *Partitur* was
prepared prior to the ultimate translation into orchestral score –
an exercise which, though labour-intensive, was for Strauss largely a
mechanical task: colour, textural and instrumental requirements
being, by that time, firmly fixed in his mind. Oddly enough the
Arabella Act 3 sketchbook contains virtually no direct indications as
to scoring, although various 'signposts' appear which undoubtedly
acted to stimulate Strauss's instrumental palette. Two outstanding
instances can be noted. The first is on p. 3 of the sketchbook (v.s.
p. 320) where, accompanying Zdenka's wild proclamation of her
intention to drown her shame in the Danube, the phrase 'Donau
Wellenbesorgung' (a need for Danube wave effects) appears above
rushing semi-quaver figurations on the stave – a direction cancelled,
'Schluß der Wellenbesorgung', at the bottom of the succeeding page.
Similarly, on p. 12 (Fig. 105, v.s. p. 329), the arrival of Djura and
Jankel with duelling weapons sparks off a flurry of descending demi-
semiquaver arpeggios, marked 'gliss.' (glissando) and illuminatingly
inscribed 'Säbel' (sabre) by the composer.

The employment of key for expressive, illustrative and structural
purposes has been noted as a half-conscious, half-subconscious
technique regulated by the composer's tonal-associative instincts.
Strauss's manipulation of tonality was at all times masterly and there
are several instances in the sketchbook where he 'reminds' himself of

9a   Facsimile from Strauss's sketchbook for the two final scenes (Act 3) of *Arabella*. Compare vocal score, p. 324, Fig. 99ff.

9b   Facsimile from Strauss's sketchbook for the two final scenes (Act 3) of *Arabella*. Compare vocal score, p. 332, Fig. 110ff.

the need for specific keys for specific purposes. One of these occurs on p. 11, immediately preceding the arrival of Mandryka's servants with weapons (see p. 93 above; v.s. p. 329). Mandryka's self-reproaches end on the dominant seventh chord of C, following which the composer jots down the instruction 'abbrechen dann C moll' (break off, then C minor), the resolution coming four bars later when Waldner insists on his right to satisfaction. The switch to C minor is of a piece with the Waldners' generic G minor (to which it is related), the C tonal area often being identified in Strauss's music with human failings and weaknesses. Another interesting example of tonal identification appears earlier, on p. 6 of the sketchbook, as Arabella assures Zdenka of support in her hour of need (Fig. 97[6], v.s. p. 323). 'Ich bin bei dir, ich laß dich nicht in Stich', she sings, the composed key of E♭ major, in retrospect, being queried by Strauss, who at the repetition, 'I'm on your side', inscribes 'B dur?' above the stave, a reminder that B♭ major is associated with Zdenka, to whom the word 'dir' clearly refers.

Of course, not all the suggestions in the sketches were implemented; although the completed score pays passing tribute to Zdenka's B♭ major at this point, the final version is far removed from the notebook jottings. Indeed, in contrast to p. 9, quoted above, the working displays an unwonted uncertainty. It seems likely that Strauss became aware here that he had overplayed his hand with the 'passion' *Motiv*, also used to underpin the culminating Matteo/Zdenka passage (see Plate 9a). Certainly the section was eventually revised, placing less emphasis on this distinctive idea, and so avoiding too explicit an anticipatory effect at the succeeding lyrical climax. Up to this point, and indeed for the first fifteen pages of the sketchbook, the process of composition appears to have proceeded chronologically. But Strauss once again appears to have had second thoughts as the important 'Brautwerbung kommt' climax approaches. The ascending dotted crotchet figure which was, in the event, to heighten the musico-dramatic tension at the moment when Mandryka asks a parental blessing on Matteo and Zdenka, arrives prematurely on page 15 (see Plate 9b, bars 11–12ff). It is evident from the sparse detail in the example provided, especially when compared with the fluency of Plate 9a, that Strauss had momentarily strayed off course. Forced to double back and to rework the passage on pp. 16 and 17 (Fig. 108–110[7], v.s. pp. 331–2), the new version eventually does arrive at A♭ major (a note indicating A♭ minor being erased from the score by the composer) for Arabella's 'Zdenkerl, du bist die

Bess're von uns zweien', although via a different route and using different materials.

The Arabella/Zdenka exchanges which follow continue on the last page of the sketchbook. From here composition somewhat puzzlingly proceeds in a reverse order, proceeding inclusively from p. 46 to p. 32. This section, starting at Fig. 110[8] (v.s. p. 332) and finishing at Fig. 129[9] (v.s. p. 348) constitutes the final version of the approach to 'Brautwerbung kommt'. In this instance, the essential climax appears to have been sketched first, enabling a structural intensification to take place through repetition of the interrogatory phrase 'Was jetzt noch kommt?'. The 'Brautwerbung kommt' climax (p. 23) provides a tonal and thematic goal towards which this intermediate passage could move. In a similarly far-sighted tonal manner, Strauss needs to establish the 'post-staircase' unresolved E♭ major dominant seventh (p. 25), before tackling its approach from 'Das war sehr gut, Mandryka'. The organisation of the sketchbook material makes it clear that this whole passage, with the staircase music at its centre, was conceived with the long-range, overall tonal scheme in view. The C♭ major interpolation, disrupting resident B♭ major, by virtue of its very out-of-context tonal nature, is able to move freely, through a wide range of apparently unrelated keys, in an emotive, intense tonal sequence which progresses by degrees back towards E♭ rehabilitation at the B♭ caesura on p. 25 (Fig. 144, v.s. p. 357).

Such glimpses into a composer's workshop are always rewarding and instructive. By such means one is able to approach more closely the mystery of the creative process. The sketch books reaffirm the remarkable intellectual grasp that Strauss had over his materials and confirm the exceptional spontaneity of his melodic gifts. 'I am not blessed with long melodies as Mozart was, I only get as far as short themes. But what I do know is how to turn a theme, paraphrase it, extract everything that is in it, and I believe nobody today can do this as well as I can',[3] remarked Strauss once to Stefan Zweig; and these sketches testify to the symphonic composer's craft. Such skill is immediately apparent in the transformation and extension of the musical ideas; but above all, the sketches confirm the powerful grasp which this composer had of large-scale musical forms. It is in his ability to relate and to integrate melodic and tonal detail into the grand structural design and in the clarity of his dramatic vision that his ultimate greatness lay. The *Arabella* sketch books remain, as indeed does the opera itself, a testimonial to these exceptional powers.

Progress towards the completion and performance of *Arabella* was less than purposeful; nonetheless, in comparison with previous works, the time between the start of composition and the Dresden premiere (just over three years) was not excessive.[1] The desolation Strauss experienced following Hofmannsthal's death, however, had something of a retarding influence, with repercussions on the destiny of the work. Elisabeth Schumann, his neighbour at Garmisch, recalls how he sought refuge in her home soon after the event. Here, fugitive from his wife's deliberately stringent and 'protective' regime, which forbade attendance at his friend's funeral, which discouraged all mention of his loss and prescribed work as the only effective remedy for grief, he was able to speak freely of Hofmannsthal and to read the *Arabella* libretto to a small group of sympathetic friends. Embarrassed as she was on this occasion by a houseful of guests, she drew off the company, leaving him alone with her husband, Karl Alwin, and the von Frankensteins.[2]

When she returned a few hours later, Strauss had gone, and the three privileged listeners told with much feeling how the composer had suddenly stopped during the reading and burst into floods of tears. He had wept long and unrestrainedly, tears forced from the very depths of his soul. Grief for the loss of the friend, having been forcibly suppressed, had found a violent outlet denied to it in his home.[3]

Now, robbed as Strauss was of the important stimulation provided by collaborative discussion and argument, the process of artistic achievement, sadly for posterity, passed with only the minimum of comment. It would be wrong to suggest that the composer had disciplined himself to undertake an uncongenial task or that he was unhappy with the libretto. Letters of the period record no evidence of dissatisfaction; rather the contrary, for in July 1929, a month after the poet's death, Strauss comments in a letter to Clemens Krauss, 'I am now already enthusiastically at work on Arabella,'[4] and on 21

September, with the rider that 'Hofmannsthal's glorious text composes as smoothly as butter!',[5] he was able to tell the Viennese critic Ludwig Karpath that the sketches for Act 1 were completed.

It would also be wrong to assume that the interruption caused by work on a modern performing edition of Mozart's *Idomeneo* reflected a loss of interest in *Arabella*. This task had been the subject of detailed discussion with Clemens Krauss well before Hofmannsthal's death; an act of homage to the beloved Mozart typical of the man who twenty years earlier had rediscovered *Così fan tutte* for twentieth-century audiences. In a letter to Krauss of June 1929,[6] he confirms his intention to commence serious work on the Mozart project the following spring, a necessary expedient if the premiere, scheduled for the Vienna Staatsoper in April 1931, was to take place according to plan. The project reached completion in the autumn of 1930, but it was not until later the following year that Strauss was able to tell Krauss, Karpath and Busch that the *Arabella* sketches for Act 3 were ready.[7] It is a commonly held belief that the disruption caused by the *Idomeneo* 'interlude' was responsible for certain stylistic 'inconsistencies' which have been detected following the Arabella/Mandryka meeting scenes of Act 2. The view is, however, purely conjectural; the apparent idiomatic diffuseness and the waltz 'interpolations' which characterise the act's *finale*, although much criticised, provide essential contrast of material and also have an obvious role in the establishment of a light-hearted ballroom *milieu*. Certainly there was little indication of creative languor or hesitation on the composer's part when he assured Krauss, in his letter of 17 October 1931, 'I am working fluently on *Arabella*; the third act is now also ready in sketch form.'[8]

Work now proceeded apace. The piano sketches were complete by November 1931, and by early February 1932, a report to Busch in Dresden, to whom the premiere had already been promised, confirmed the instrumentation of the first one hundred pages of the score. Now at last Strauss was in a position to forecast the date of the first performance, making the tentative suggestion of September 1933; meanwhile, the score of Act 1 reached completion on 6 March 1932, with Act 2 following exactly three months later.

Now, for the first time, an element of disillusionment creeps into his work. In November 1931, faced with the complex task of scoring the opera from the piano sketches, he had written, 'But don't ask me when the score will be ready! The times are not ripe for such a work as this: I shan't be in too much of a hurry over it.'[9] In July 1932, although only the instrumentation of the final act remained to be finished, he concedes:

It has not been easy for me to make the decision temporarily to put off the *Arabella* premiere. But in the first place I have become somewhat wearied by the effort of it all and would like to interrupt it with a new work, just as long as my powers of invention continue to function as I approach my seventieth year. Secondly, the financial circumstances (neither the publisher, the theatre nor the public has any money) have now become so difficult, that I believe it would be foolish to squander a big work in the uncertainty of the present times.[10]

The comment should be interpreted in the light of new creative developments. Strauss was now in urgent personal negotiation with the Austrian poet Stefan Zweig over a promising new operatic venture based upon Ben Jonson's comedy *The Silent Woman*. Strauss always found the summer months most congenial for composition and at present, with *Arabella* at the scoring stage, his attitude was clearly influenced by a pressing inner need for creative occupation. Instrumentation always tended to be a winter activity, and a break now, delaying *Arabella* by a predictable three months on top of the summer composing period, would indeed have rendered the projected 1933 premiere impracticable. Furthermore, one detects a new note of urgency behind Strauss's words – at sixty-eight his creative inspiration was still running strongly, but, conscious of the passage of time, he was anxious to seize every opportunity of capitalising on a diminishing asset. Nor is this the whole picture. The Reichstag elections of 31 July had produced a resounding National Socialist victory in Germany, and there were disquieting rumours abroad, especially from Dresden, where the Nazi-dominated Saxon *Landtag* was already making its presence felt in the Semperoper.[11] Despite everything, however, and largely due to the insistent prodding of Busch and Reucker, work on *Arabella* continued, the third act reaching completion on 12 October 1932.

A new opera by Richard Strauss was, of course, bound to be in demand, and considerable interest was shown by all the important German-speaking houses. Strauss was adamant that the premiere should go to Busch in Dresden (the date was now brought forward to 1 July 1933), but a diplomatic arrangement was reached at the request of Heinz Tietjen,[12] the Berlin *Intendant*, to satisfy Furtwängler, Knappertsbusch and Krauss, whereby the work would be refused general circulation until its introduction in Berlin, Munich and Vienna respectively. For this purpose a term of four months was set, up to 1 October, although Knappertsbusch, already committed to a new production of *Die ägyptische Helena* that year, which in the event took place in September, was pleading, on practical grounds, for an extension to 15 October.

When Strauss communicated these decisions to Clemens Krauss in the middle of January 1933 events appeared to be taking their prescribed course. Casting and rehearsal schedules were already under negotiation between the composer, Busch, the Dresden *Intendant*, Alfred Reucker, the repetiteur, Erich Engel and the scenic and costume designer, Leonhard Fanto. Since, as usual, Strauss kept in close contact with all those responsible for the new production, he must have been acutely aware of the tensions building up in Dresden following the appointment of Hitler as German Chancellor on 30 January 1933.

Busch relates that as early as the autumn of 1932, the personnel of the opera house had been infiltrated by Nazi spies, who, reporting his natural aversion to the régime, lost no opportunity to foment trouble, enlisting the help of the National Socialist gutter press to inflame the situation by drawing attention to his attitude of noncooperation. By February 1933, the month in which Strauss visited him in Dresden to read over the libretto of *Die schweigsame Frau*, the storm was reaching its height. On 7 March, Busch was scheduled to direct a performance of Verdi's *Rigoletto* at the Opera. A demonstration was organised by the Nazis. On that evening he was threatened and deprived of his post in favour of assistant Kapellmeister Hermann Kutzschbach, subsequently being ordered into the pit to direct the performance before an auditorium filled with SA men who hooted him from the podium. The next day Reucker was also summarily dismissed and a new *Generalintendant* of the Dresden theatres appointed, one *Geheimrat* Dr Adolph. As Busch wryly comments, 'There was no longer any doubt that the fate of the Dresden Opera and the future of Art in the Third Reich were now in the best hands.'[13]

Even as late as February 1933, Strauss had met Busch and Tietjen in Berlin to discuss the *Arabella* premiere, and had at that time made his position absolutely clear; the work would only be released for Dresden if the performance remained in the hands of the dedicatees. If, under the circumstances, Busch refused to direct, then the venue would have to be changed. Unfortunately, the affair had by now become something of a *cause célèbre* in the eyes of the Nazi administration who were not prepared to suffer the loss of face, both national and international, that would result from the withdrawal of a new work by the world's foremost operatic composer. Nevertheless, despite mounting pressure, Strauss, writing to Krauss on 27 March 1933, still insists that without the collaboration of Reucker, Busch and Engel, any prospect of a premiere on 1 July is out of the question.[14] Oddly enough, in the same letter, there are signs of faltering resolution on the part of the composer, who had, it appears, already approved the feelers Tietjen had put out to ascertain the extent of Krauss's availability for Dresden. Hints of behind-the-scenes negotiations can be clearly sensed in the timely warning that Strauss issued to his colleague:

For the present some friendly advice, don't commit yourself to Dresden in any way! Should the administration there, who apparently aren't always *au fait* with developments in Berlin, approach you directly with an invitation, use me as an excuse, as one whose 'agreement in principle you must first secure'. In this manner the Dresden affair can be stalled until Tietjen gives the go-ahead.[15]

Clearly Tietjen, as Reichstheater mogul, and incidentally as a longstanding friend and colleague of Strauss, had instructions from the government to sort things out, the whole business being complicated by the insistence of the Dresden Opera management upon the exact legal terms of their contract. There was obviously little room for manoeuvre, and Strauss's unenviable situation can be accurately gauged from correspondence of the time. On 4 April writing to Fanto, on receipt of a conciliatory and apparently favourable off-the-cuff assurance on the legal situation via Tietjen from Adolph in Dresden, he comments:

He (Adolph) remembers the great days of Dresden and understands the significance of a Strauss premiere under Schuch. Of all people therefore he will realise that *Arabella* for 1 July is no longer possible. For months Reucker, Busch, Engel and you have wrestled with the very special difficulties of the work and the artistic personnel responsible for a premiere on 1 July, ought from this moment onward to be constantly occupied with it, or at least to be supervising the production. I would welcome a situation whereby the excellent Clemens Krauss could direct Arabella on 1 July: but there would have to be a precondition, that he immediately, wherever possible together with Wallerstein, definitely joins the Dresden opera team. But even if he promised exclusively to devote the period from 1 June (the latest possible date) up to the middle of July, to Dresden, he could hardly honour such a commitment while he still retained the directorship of the Vienna Staatsoper, which also holds its festival weeks in June. In addition, as far as casting the work is concerned, so far we have found neither a Mandryka, an Elemer nor a Waldner. . .Thus July is impossible. This disruption to your festival plans saddens me greatly; but it is not my fault. Whether I can honour my pledge in respect of the Dresden premiere for the autumn, must depend (and this the great Schuch worshipper Adolph will certainly appreciate) on the composition of the new musical administration in Dresden. You, dear Fanto, best know the difficulties of *Arabella* which we have discussed at length in conference with Reucker, Busch and Engel, and you can understand that the performance of the work under a conductor who does not have my complete confidence would be neither advantageous for Dresden nor, to me personally, pleasurable.[16]

Strauss enclosed a copy of this letter, to Krauss, a few days later, commenting that Dresden was at all costs still determined to keep to the announced festival programme, including *Arabella*, despite the stupid hounding out of Busch, the only man capable of fulfilling all the essential requirements. Confirming once again the difficulties of casting the work, he points out that his primary concern is not merely with the premiere and its immediate aftermath, but with its long-term prospects:

For the real success of *Arabella* it is much more important that the work remains throughout the following winter in the hands of the person who was responsible for the premiere – and he must be a first class conductor. Until I know who that is going to be I can certainly decide nothing. You will thus without further ado understand why I must turn down *every* guest conductor for July (even one called Clemens Krauss) in the interest of *Arabella*'s future. It would be quite another thing if you could completely devote yourself to Dresden during the autumn. However, if such a happy prospect were to present itself, I could no longer sanction what would in the present circumstances be a hasty and precipitate premiere on 1 July! Too late is simply too late! This is also Tietjen's view![17]

In spite of this apparent intransigence, before the end of the month some sort of settlement had been reached between Strauss and Dresden, as well as a compromise agreement with Krauss over his Viennese commitments. On 20 April, a brief communication from Garmisch[18] summoned the conductor to a meeting in Munich, assuring him that everything had been sorted out in a personal confrontation with Adolph – 'Our discussion will not take very long!', he asserts – and it is clear from now on that Krauss was to consider himself responsible for the premiere, which, despite the composer's earlier misgivings, was once more firmly fixed for 1 July. The manipulative *Geheimrat* Adolph had achieved his ends and satisfied his masters – Nazi 'diplomacy' had triumphed.

It is not clear what particular pressures were brought to bear upon Strauss in order to effect a result so diametrically opposed to his professional instincts and personal inclinations. One is, however, aware of the conciliatory attitudes adopted by the Nazis toward prominent figures in the Reich whom they wished to exploit for propaganda purposes. Strauss's devotion to German music and his championship of musicians' rights was well known, and both hard and deductive evidence suggests that the authorities cunningly held out promises for the future which, worthless and empty as they proved to be, convinced the politically naïve composer that improvements and new opportunities were on the way. 'I have brought back from Berlin', he writes to the sceptical Kippenberg[19] at the end of March 1933, 'great impressions and real hopes for the future of German Art once the first throes of the revolutionary storm have subsided.'[20] Such a bait as the imminent formation of the Reichsmusikkammer, holding out great potential for necessary and beneficial reform, of which Strauss was to be appointed president in November 1933, might also have been thrown out in the effort to persuade him to compromise on the Dresden situation. Indeed all the signs suggest that a supreme effort, marshalling all the forces of apparent reasonableness, was mounted by the Nazi administration in their successful attempt to exploit the unsuspecting composer and to bend him to their purpose.

Practically speaking, arrangements worked out as follows. Krauss reduced his commitment to the Vienna Festival significantly during June 1933, in order to devote as much time as possible to Dresden. In addition, it was decided to offer the role of Arabella to the Dresden-contracted Viorica Ursuleac who also frequently sang under Krauss's baton in Vienna. His close personal relationship with Ursuleac,[21] and the decision to invite the Viennese baritone Alfred Jerger to create Mandryka in both the Dresden and Viennese premieres proved a clever expedient which was both artistically satisfactory and also destined to streamline preliminary preparations, which could now be undertaken, conveniently for Krauss, on the spot in the Austrian capital.

Back in Dresden, the musical preliminaries were in the hands of Leo Wurmser, the chief repetiteur, and Kutzschbach, who subsequently took over from Krauss and for whom, as an erstwhile colleague of Busch, Strauss evidently had considerable respect.[22] Considering the limited time (little over a month) that was available for rehearsal, it is hardly surprising that, at the composer's request, his first Octavian, the veteran Dresden soprano Eva von der Osten (now married to Friedrich Platschke, who was to sing Waldner), was brought in in an advisory capacity on the stage direction side – an unprecedented but obviously practical move. The producer was Josef Gielen.[23]

Naturally all the resources of the Dresden opera house were mobilised. The cast had been made up by Platschke (Waldner), Kallab (Adelaide) and Streib (Elemer) – all last-minute appointments – most of the other roles having already been decided upon during the Busch era. Strauss attended all the rehearsals, according to Ursuleac, who confirms the occasion as

A unique experience. . .The theatre was simply shut down for three weeks and rehearsals went on from early morning until late into the night. Everyone, right down to the meanest stage hand, was inspired by the work, an unforgettable period and its success was fabulous.[24]

The Dresden periodical *Das schöne Sachsen* describes the scene on the evening of 1 July:

For weeks people in musical circles have been able to talk about nothing else. In Dresden no effort was spared to ensure that the day of the premiere would become a festival for Richard Strauss and his music. The opera was, despite considerably increased prices, sold out days before the performance, reservations for tickets being received from all over the world. An audience of rare distinction filled the auditorium. The *Reichsstatthalter* was seated in the middle of the dress circle along with uniformed ministers while the composer and his family savoured the occasion, in full view of everyone, from a nearby box. Wherever one looked one glimpsed the famous and influential – the popular lyric poet Hanns Jobst, Max von Schillings, Furtwängler, the Crown Prince Reuss (the theatre prince), the family of Hugo von Hofmannsthal, national and local government representatives, officers, diplomats, musicians and theatre personnel. The house was wonderfully tense as the director of the Vienna Opera, guest conductor Clemens Krauss, took his place on the rostrum. There was, contrary to Dresden custom, continuous applause after a duet in the middle of the first act, indicative of a desire on the audience's part to force an encore. After the rousing second act one asked oneself whether Strauss and Hofmannsthal would be able to rise to an even greater climax in the third. As the curtain rose yet again, however, all present felt after a few moments that in the dramatically practical, picturesque atmosphere of the hotel vestibule all the best and most spiritual theatrical ingredients had been assembled. There were new dramatic tensions, new musical highlights and the work ended with a storm of approval such as has seldom been demonstrated in the history of operatic first performances. Again and again the artists were called back on to the stage, in their midst the modest, youthful-looking Master Strauss, already about to embark upon the seventieth year of his life.[25]

Strauss himself was particularly pleased, although not a little surprised by the success of the work. 'What a pity that you couldn't be there', he writes to Karpath a few days after the performance, continuing, 'The *Arabella* premiere was a particular triumph for the Viennese singers Ursuleac and Jerger. Clemens Krauss conducted so well that, according to the old Viennese tradition, it must be about time to get rid of him!'[26] Karpath had, in fact, managed to catch a radio broadcast of the work and after sadly pointing out that this was the first Strauss premiere he had missed since *Feuersnot*, assured the master of the pleasure the performance had given him. 'Such a wonderful work will do much to restore the fortunes of the Vienna opera', he commented, concluding by wishing the composer many more successes along the lines of 'This masterly Arabella, at long last and above all, a work which makes one feel good inside'.[27]

The Viennese premiere, produced by Lothar Wallerstein[28] and once again directed by Clemens Krauss, was, if anything, even more of a success. Perhaps because of the work's setting the *Kaiserstadt* took it to its heart. The veteran stage designer Alfred Roller provided 'classically' authentic solutions for both the first and final acts, utilising for the second, on grounds of economy, existing material culled from Heuberger's unsuccessful *Ein Opernball* of 1931. The occasion was also marked by a burst of affection from the sentimental Viennese public for Lotte Lehmann, who, in spite of receiving news of the death of her mother that same evening, gave a radiant performance in the title role, which, according to Joseph Marx, she enhanced by 'the grace of her appearance and the magic of her vocal art'.[29]

It was an experience I shall never forget. No power in the world is greater than that of music. For two brief hours it enabled me to forget my deep personal grief, to be Arabella rather than my own tormented, pain-racked, and mourning self. . .how grateful I was for that premiere. Strauss, profoundly touched by my consent to go ahead and sing, wanted to take me out with him to the footlights at the end of the performance, but I had to refuse. . .thus Strauss himself stepped out and announced that he would accept the thanks of the audience on behalf of Lotte Lehmann.[30]

Not surprisingly under the circumstances, Ursuleac deputised for Lehmann in the next four Viennese *Arabella*s, subsequently sharing the current run of performances in the ratio of twelve to five with her illustrious colleague, while Luise Helletsgruber alternated with Margit Bokor, the Dresden Zdenka, who had now, at Krauss's instigation, been offered a Vienna contract. These were the only significant casting changes to take place in a production which, apart from Jerger, also included Richard Mayr as Waldner, Helga Roswaenge as Matteo, Josef Kalenberg as Elemer, and Adele Kern as Fiakermilli. All the performances took place under Krauss's baton – save that of

20 December, 1933, when Josef Krips took over due to the illness of his chief – the final staging being on 9 November 1934, shortly before Krauss left Vienna for Berlin.

Furtwängler's Berlin *Arabella* took place on the same evening as the Viennese premiere, with Viorica Ursuleac repeating her Dresden triumph of the summer months. It was, indeed, this opera, performances of which took her all over Europe, that consolidated her international reputation; of particular note being her appearances in London in May 1934 with Krauss, and in Amsterdam on 29 November that same year under the composer's own baton. *Arabella*'s future was, it seems, secure enough as far as German-speaking countries were concerned, but its reception abroad was less enthusiastic. For this, the political climate was undoubtedly to some extent to blame, and it can be no accident that in Budapest and London in 1934, the Hungarian and British press demonstrated a sharply critical attitude, whereas in fascist Italy performances in 1936 (the Strauss/Wallerstein/Jerger team) and 1937, at Genoa and Trieste respectively, were more warmly received.

Indeed, apart from a few productions in Buenos Aires under Busch, and in French in Monte Carlo in 1934,[31] *Arabella*'s international appeal, as the political situation developed, proved, predictably enough, to be somewhat restricted. It was otherwise in Germany itself where Clemens Krauss, who demonstrated and professed a great love for the work, was in an excellent position to champion its progress. Already singled out by Strauss, 'Papst Clemens' was soon, with the composer's encouragement and support, to achieve an unassailable and influential position in German music. Succeeding Furtwängler in Berlin in March 1935, in that same year he directed his first Berlin *Arabella*. In 1937, he was appointed *Intendant* of the Munich Staatsoper where, in 1939, he undertook a completely new staging of the work, in collaboration with Rudolph Hartmann, which with the composer's approval, incorporating certain cuts, also amalgamated the two final acts in an effort to strengthen the overall dramatic concept.

This, the famous so-called 'Munich version' of the work, has had an unfortunate effect upon subsequent performances of the opera, many of which, ostensibly adopting what they believed to be an 'accepted' and acceptable 'improvement', have made the Krauss/Hartmann experiments an excuse for devastating cuts in the sensitively balanced third act. Hartmann himself has, since the war, specifically advocated such practices, and explicitly states in his book on the staging of the Strauss operas that Strauss 'agreed without hesitation to a fusion of the second and third acts (with abridgements of Act III) when this was suggested by Clemens Krauss for a new production of the work at Munich in 1939'.[32] However, Dr Götz-Klaus Kende, who has Krauss's own scores available in the Clemens Krauss Archive in Vienna, asserts that

Clemens Krauss simply made a few tiny cuts in Act 2. . .In the third act he *never* made any cuts at all. Rudolph Hartmann's memory has played him false when he speaks of abridgements in Act 3! The usual barbaric cuts in today's performances of the final act, which rob Arabella of some of her most beautiful and most important lines, are a product of later times. . .[33]

Dr Kende's comments are of considerable importance in view of the liberties so often taken with the *Arabella* score today when it is very rare indeed to hear anything approaching a full performance of the work. The Munich Festival under Sawallisch in 1977 went some way towards redressing the balance of Keilberth's earlier ruthless treatment, while in England, it appears, the nearest approach to a complete *Arabella* was the Dresden staging under Krauss in 1934. The Bavarian State Opera visit of 1953 with Kempe was produced by Hartmann, as was the Solti Covent Garden production of 1965, which, although employing the original three-act division, still made huge excisions in Act 3, as did later revivals up to the 1980s. The Haitink/Cox production (Glyndebourne 1984) was also culpable in this respect but another three-act version in 1984, that of the English National Opera, whilst circumspectly omitting some of the problematic Fiakermilli music of Act 2, at least restored the important passage from Fig. 110[7] to Fig. 119 in the score. This comprises ninety-three bars of glorious music as well as some twenty-four lines of text, without which the technical devices and subtleties of characterisation leading up to Mandryka's forgiveness and the tension-releasing 'Brautwerbung kommt' are simply lost.

The cuts and alterations originally made by Krauss for Munich 1939 may be identified as follows:

Act 2 Fig. 105[8]–6 (episode between Dominik and Adelaide). 14 bars
Fig. 120[5]–1 (Fiakermilli coloratura). 5 bars
Fig. 130–2 (Fiakermilli/Mandryka). 37 bars[34]

The transition into Act 3 was effected from Fig. 148 directly into the opening bars of the introduction to the last act. Fig. 147 remains, but the last chord before Fig. 148 is transposed one tone higher –

from the Db major dominant seventh to the Eb major dominant – the resolution of which to the E major of the Act 3 prelude constitutes a common and characteristically Straussian progression.

Krauss was, of course, tireless in his suggestions to Strauss for the 'improvement' of his works, and, to be fair, his requests were always made with some valid musical or dramatic point in mind. It says much for Strauss's confidence in his judgement and musical abilities, born of a long personal and professional association and represented by a correspondence covering a period of twenty-two years, that he apparently never resented, and usually acquiesced in, the often fundamental changes which his colleague proposed.[35] As we have already observed, the Fiakermilli figure had always been a thorn in Krauss's flesh and in 1942 during preparation for a revival of the opera at the Salzburg Festival of that year, he proposed alterations which required the composer to alter radically her light-hearted opening ditty:

> My proposition is as follows: the Fiakermilli couplet in 3/4 time must have two stanzas, the second with an introductory ritornello to begin at Figure 42. At the end of each verse a short choral refrain (repeating the text). The second verse should move directly (without the yodelling cadenza!) into the waltz, three beats before Figure 45 (cutting out the intervening chorus).[36]

The required additional text, Krauss believed, might be salvaged from discarded portions of Hofmannsthal's original script but failing that, he undertook, with Hartmann's help, to provide the necessary lines himself.[37] The result was a second stanza upon which the composer's revision was based. Broadly following Krauss's suggestions the final bars of the existing *Lied* were recast, their repetition supplying a choral refrain, before subsequent adaptation of the melody to fit the words of the new second verse. The revised score supplied to Krauss reveals some ambiguity over Strauss's intentions respecting Fiakermilli's cadenza, whose fate he was presumably content to leave in the conductor's hands. It may be assumed that these changes were incorporated, according to design, in the 1942 Salzburg Festival performances, along with certain other orchestral readjustments requested by Krauss[38] to enhance the ballroom atmosphere of the second act. While it is doubtful whether this revision has ever been performed, except by Krauss, its melodic rationalisations, heightening the effect of the Fiakermilli entrance scene, greatly enhance the drama, presenting an option which, considering the views Strauss expressed at this time,[39] presumably represent his final thoughts on the matter. Krauss's last performance of the opera took place in 1944 at Salzburg in honour of Strauss's eightieth birthday celebrations, completing a life-time total of sixty-five performances of a work upon which he had placed his own irrevocable interpretative stamp.

Naturally enough, after the war, opera was slow to recover from a devastation which had eliminated many of the most important opera houses in Europe.[40] It was Karl Böhm who reintroduced *Arabella* to Salzburg in 1947, in a production by Günter Rennert and designed by Robert Kautsky. This performance, fortunately preserved on disc, with Maria Reining as Arabella, Hans Hotter as Mandryka, Georg Hann as Waldner and Lisa Della Casa as Zdenka, forges an interesting link between the pre-war Krauss tradition (Hotter and Hann had both sung the work at Munich in 1939) and post-war developments. Della Casa's wonderfully fresh-sounding and intelligent Zdenka immediately established her as a Strauss singer *par excellence*, whilst in her later 'classic' portrayal of Arabella, her glorious purity of tone and her inspired interpretative and human sensitivity persuaded at least one critic that she was 'absolutely predestined for this role',[41] others coining the term '*Arabellissima*' to describe her triumph. Indeed, the Solti Vienna recording, which stems from this period, indicates just how much she had inherited, in terms of timing and dramatic inflection, from the veteran Reining, whose experience of the part dated back to the Viennese performances of 1937.

The success of this work rests first and foremost upon the portrayal of a title role which calls for rare physical grace as well as an exceptional combination of singing and acting ability. All the great executants of the role have possessed such attributes. Ursuleac, of course, contributed crucially to the fortunes of the opera in Germany during the thirties and forties. Lotte Lehmann's unique and authentic study, only glimpsed in recorded excerpts, was sadly cut short by voluntary political exile – ultimately in the United States, where the work was not premiered until 1955. In Europe, the advent of the incomparable Della Casa played an important part in restoring the opera to the repertoire. Her 1952 Viennese debut in the title role, the first *Arabella* in the Austrian capital for eight years, and its subsequent preservation by Decca, had a crucial effect upon the work's fortunes. From this time forward, *Arabella* has featured more consistently in performances world-wide, although it still achieves its greatest popularity in the German-speaking countries.

Less favourable reception elsewhere probably stems from the lingering effect of pre-war criticism which, particularly in English-speaking countries, many commentators seem unable or unwilling to shake off. Perhaps for this reason the work has been treated in a somewhat cavalier fashion, although, surprisingly enough, those savage cuts already noted in British performances have been authenticated abroad, even in the Bavarian Strauss heartland of Munich. The live Bavarian State Opera recording under Keilberth, employing the Munich version, has extensive cuts in Acts 2 and 3; while the more recent Sawallisch discs of 1981, apparently a studio 'take' of the Munich Opera production of 1977 (revived in 1983 with a new cast, but once more condensed into two acts), goes some way towards the restoration of Bavarian honour in this respect.

For the first time in living memory the opera is heard in its entirety, uncut. The wounds which had hitherto been inflicted upon the score, even in Munich itself, are healed. In the second and third acts one views scenes and hears music which previously one simply didn't know existed. Now the plot is once more complete, now at last the proportions of the act are correct. '*Zdenkerl, du bist die bessere von uns zweien*', Arabella now sings in the third act. This, never before heard, is however, characterwise, at least as important as her steadfast determination to wait for the man of her dreams who will, one day, stand at her side.[42]

Despite this, Solti's 1957 recording remained the only absolutely complete *Arabella* available on disc for thirty years,[43] although a further uncut performance under the same conductor with Gundula Janowitz in the title role, is preserved in the British Library Sound Archive. Janowitz, indeed, is one of those rare and distinguished artists specifically and triumphantly identified with this exacting role, while a younger generation of singers, including Ashley Putnam, Kiri Te Kanawa and Felicity Lott hold out a great deal of potential for the future.

In terms of stage production the tale is simpler to relate. So exact were Hofmannsthal's instructions regarding decor, and so crucial to the *milieu* of the work is its Viennese atmosphere, that *Arabella* has largely escaped the self-aggrandising follies of producers. However, the not always successful but increasingly common practice of inviting a film or television producer into the opera house brought Peter Beauvais to Munich in 1977 with much-criticised results. His attempt at social comment accentuated the poverty of the Waldners in Act 1, whilst the second act was set in a seedy second-class venue in the Vienna *Vorstadt* rather than the splendid surroundings tradition dictates for the *Fiakerball*. Beauvais, taking his cue from earlier, subsequently discarded versions of the text, was deliberately chancing his arm here, since the collaborative correspondence, as well as the poet's stage directions, confirm that something more sumptuous, perhaps along the lines of the *Fledermaus* second-act setting, was looked for.

In this instance Beauvais's concept, without over-stepping the bounds of reasonableness, hardly enhanced the spirit of Strauss's music. A more recent experiment in Kiel in 1987, deploying the second act as a masked ball, proved as disastrous as it was unnecessary. The fantastic mask of Mandryka's 'angel' as she 'stepped down from heaven', making nonsense of his outspoken reverence of her beauty, made the audience laugh.[44] Nevertheless despite some minor hiccups, a splendidly consistent feature of *Arabella* productions over the course of the last thirty years has been a wide range of beautiful sets, of which a number are described and illustrated in Hartmann's book.[45] During this time, despite severe censure in some quarters and a fair degree of scepticism in others, the opera has held its own and even given signs of gaining ground, not only in the affection of audiences, by whom it has always been accorded a warm reception, but also amongst the critics, who are, it seems, at last coming to terms with the unique, pioneering qualities of this graceful 'Lyrical Comedy'.

10   Clemens Krauss on his way to the rostrum at the Vienna Staatsoper in the 1930s. Krauss was, apart from directing the *Arabella*
premiere, particularly associated with this opera throughout his
career. His final performance took place at the Salzburg Festival of
1944, in honour of Strauss's eightieth birthday.

11 From right to left: Richard Strauss, Lothar Wallerstein (producer), Lotte Lehmann (Arabella) and Alfred Jerger (Mandryka), following the Viennese premiere of *Arabella* in October 1933. Jerger had created the Mandryka role in Dresden earlier that same year.

12 Viorica Ursuleac (creator of the Arabella role), with Maud Cunitz (Zdenka), during

13   Lisa Della Casa and Anny Felbermayer (Arabella
and Zdenka) at the 1952 Vienna revival of *Arabella*

14   Lisa Della Casa in the final scene of *Arabella*, Vienna, 1952. This performance earned her the epithet '*Arabellissima*' from the critics.

9 Critical reactions

Strauss's music, it appears, has always aroused controversy; indeed, so long and fruitful a career, moving through so many phases and encompassing such spectacular triumphs, was bound to attract criticism. A disappointed *avant garde* had deprecated his achievement in *Der Rosenkavalier*, despite, or as the result of, its success and popular appeal. For the critics, Strauss's reputation seems never fully to have recovered from this apparent betrayal of the twentieth century musical aesthetic, the effect of which was perhaps more acutely observed outside Germany. An Englishman, Neville Cardus, writing in the 1950s, sums up this hard-line attitude, defining, in *Arabella*'s relationship to the earlier work, a critical stance still prevalent:

For several years Strauss has had a belittling press in this country in certain quarters, where romanticism has been attacked with a petulant wistfulness, for reasons doubtless as much psychological as aesthetic. *Arabella* was dismissed at its first performance in London nearly twenty years ago as a pale imitation of *Rosenkavalier*. I cannot resist saving my face in this connection by quoting from my notice of this first performance at Covent Garden, printed publicly on 18th May 1934: 'Up to a point *Arabella* is charming enough with instrumentation as stylish and more light-fingered than anything Strauss has ever done before. The tissue is often beautifully woven; there are taste and poise in the orchestra, and plenty of lovely sounds. *Arabella* is proof that Strauss is still the best composer of a Strauss opera.[1]

Cardus was not alone in his opinion. By the early fifties, a less politically charged atmosphere prevailed than in the 1930s, and greater familiarity with the work promoted a more informed reassessment. A repentant Ernest Newman, in the context of the London visit of the Bavarian State Opera under Kempe in 1953, made public recantation:

The present performances are of particular interest to me, if only for the reason that they are helping me to reconsider some of the opinions of the later Strauss operas which I used to express in the thirties. . .I freely confess that I myself sadly misjudged the work [*Arabella*] in 1934, and various friends whom I have sounded have also admitted gladly that their former patronising attitude towards the opera has now been radically changed. What were the reasons for our underrating of it? One of them may possibly have been that the performances we heard in 1934 were not so good as that of last Tuesday, though of this, of course, we cannot be sure. A more fundamental reason certainly was that we made the age-old mistake of listening to a new work in the wrong way. *Arabella* had for us at that time too many superficial correspondencies with the *Rosenkavalier* – the girl Zdenka masquerading as a boy (in the *Rosenkavalier* it had been the other way round): the irruption into the Vienna scene of a semi-rustic feudal lord (Mandryka) from the wilds of Croatia bringing with him, though in a different way, the odour of the fields as Baron Ochs had done; the long scena for the heroine alone at the end of the first act, which seemed to the unwary listener of 1934 to be infringing the copyright of the Marschallin's great monologue at the end of the first act of the earlier work; the occasional waltzes; and so on. On the purely musical side we were aware of too many of the Straussian 'finger-prints' which the earlier masterpiece had engraved on our minds. We were so much and so wrongly preoccupied with spotting the surface resemblances with the *Rosenkavalier* that we were deaf and blind to most of what we can now see was new and most admirable in *Arabella* – the rare delicacy of much of the psychological and musical line-drawing, the quiet art with which what is in large part essentially a conversation piece was worked out.[2]

Newman was right to discount the real or imagined inadequacies of those earlier performances. Stefan Zweig, with the text of *Die schweigsame Frau* already under his belt, and self-exiled in London, had attended the Covent Garden premiere on 17 May 1934, and wrote to the composer of the 'truly extraordinary spontaneity and warmth' of its reception, 'rising toward the end to quite un-English enthusiasm'. He went on to say, 'The direction by Erhardt, as well as the decor, were significantly better than in Vienna – clearer, simpler, livelier – and Clemens Krauss has long since earned for himself the Grand Cross of the Richard Strauss Order.'[3] Despite Zweig's favourable impressions, press reviews of these performances were less than enthusiastic. 'Since the subject is a comedy of Viennese society, the opera-goer is naturally inclined to ask, has Strauss achieved a second *Rosenkavalier*?' So wrote the *Times* correspondent, going on to complain that 'The first impression of the opera as a whole is that the composer repeats in it a manner to which he has long been accustomed and does so with only partial success.'[4]

While reports twenty years later are generally mellower, they still show wide differences of opinion, ranging from downright condemnation to whole-hearted acceptance. *The Times*, for instance, was unchangingly dismissive:

The general verdict [in 1934] was that it was the mixture, Strauss and von Hofmannsthal, as before, shaken up with slight changes in the quantities of the ingredients. Zerbinetta from *Ariadne* had been dropped diluted into the recipe for *Der Rosenkavalier*. It was deduced that Strauss had written himself out, that his cynical worldliness had hardened upon him. The facts were right, but the deduction, in the light of history, has been proved wrong. What was worked out was the collaboration with von Hofmannsthal who, in fact, did not live to hear the opera. Instead of the Vienna of Maria Theresa we are given the Vienna of Franz Josef, instead of the palaces of the aristocracy a hotel of the bourgeoisie, instead of a silver rose a glass of cold water. Not all the Nine Muses together could grant anything so contrary to nature as an imitation surpassing its original. And *Arabella* remains, for all the skill and experience of master-craftsmen that have gone into it, second-rate stuff,'[5]

This was counteracted by the *Guardian*'s Philip Hope-Wallace, who, reporting on 'the warmest and most humane of his [Strauss's] operas after *Rosenkavalier*', also comments, 'It takes getting to know. I find that even after five *Arabella*'s, points in the give and take of the dialogue escape me.' 'Some people were bored', he continues, 'But whoever took in *Rosenkavalier* at first hearing?'[6] The same paper drew attention to the relative weakness of the second act *finale*, but also pointed out that the waltz sequences which establish the ballroom atmosphere are stylistically appropriate in their 1860s setting, whereas in the baroque *milieu* of *Rosenkavalier* they can, for all their nostalgic charm, only be described as anachronistic. In the event most commentaries from 1953 onwards reflect Lisa Della Casa's impact in the title role, and record, in common with contemporary Continental reviews, the beginning of a more objective postwar reassessment of the work.

No doubt, English criticism of the 1930s, influenced by anti-German sentiment, was to some extent a reaction to popular opinion abroad. In German-speaking countries, of course, *Arabella* was greeted with warmth, the 'highlights' of the score in particular arousing unqualified approval everywhere:

Without doubt it is Strauss's music that invests the libretto with a live theatrical presence. . .His powers of musical characterisation are incomparable – we see them deftly defined in the opening card scene which anticipates the entire dramatic development of the work, in the evocative sketch of the forest with its gipsies, charcoal-burners, bears and deer, which Mandryka has bartered for funds to enable him to visit Arabella, and in the brilliantly lucid portrayal of each new figure in turn as it appears upon the scene. The noble warmth of Straussian melody in the brief, inspired, duet outpourings of the first and second acts, Arabella's incredible solo scene, and Mandryka's marvellous D major *Ariette*. . .culminate in the third act *finale*, as Arabella

slowly descends the staircase towards her repentant and reconciled lover. . .
a simple thread of Croatian folksong is woven into the gold-glistening
Straussian orchestral tapestry with its broad, sweeping melodic arches of
such unutterable beauty. Admittedly the waltzes which create a thoroughly
appropriate, pleasing and light-hearted ball-room atmosphere, pale against
those of *Der Rosenkavalier*; whilst much of the textually long drawn out and
diffuse second act – even we who have revered and admired the beloved
master since childhood have to admit it – is characterised more by skill and
craftsmanship than by intrinsic artistic quality. Nevertheless, we have here a
masterpiece which diverts us, for the duration of two short hours, by conjur-
ing up an appealing, if lost, world, through the skill of two great practi-
tioners of the operatic art.[7]

It is not surprising, given Hofmannsthal's rank as a writer and
poet, that some attention should have been paid to this posthumous
text, which aroused a great deal of interest in both literary and
musical circles. Joseph Gregor praised the work as 'The most successful of the partners' collaborative efforts', referring to Hofmannsthal's 'wonderful array of poetic characters', and specifically defining Arabella and Zdenka as 'marvellously theatrical figures'.[8] Generally speaking, however, despite acclaim for the music, there was
limited praise for the 'book'. While the Swiss critic Hans Schnoor
hailed the poet's 'melodically characteristic, beautiful and strangely
evocative verse with its rich well-rounded style and cadence',[9] the
Viennese Joseph Marx castigated Hofmannsthal for what he saw
as an unsuccessful attempt, through the introduction of 'noticeably
sloppy' linguistic habits, to lend a naturally 'wienerisch' tone and
inflection to the dialogue. 'Apparently everything in this work that
impresses the listener by its feeling, depths, character or atmosphere',
he wrote, 'stems from Strauss, not from Hofmannsthal'.[10] The Hungarian periodical *A Zene*, reporting on the Budapest premiere of
1935, dismissed the entire proceedings:

It was an even greater surprise to us that director Rednai had, with little hope
of success, built this burdensome work of Richard Strauss into his programme. One can scarcely hail this posthumous piece by Hofmannsthal as
an ideal opera libretto. Although as a distinguished man of the theatre he
well understands how to entertain the public with deft and diverting scenes,
we look here in vain for those signs of inspirational depths and poetic genius
which characterise his best work.[11]

These early judgments set a critical tone which still exerts some
influence today. But during the last twenty years, scholarly reassessment has initiated a reversal of the earlier cavalier treatment
accorded to Hofmannsthal's text. Indeed, opinion over this period

demonstrates something of a turnabout in this respect, the virtually unfailing admiration for Strauss's music up to the fifties now being tempered by a considerably greater awareness (undoubtedly influenced by the updating of the Strauss/Hofmannsthal correspondences in 1955)[12] of the uniqueness of his partner's achievement. The extreme view – inclining to place the merit of what *The Daily Telegraph* once described as 'an improbably trivial text'[13] over the now popularly observed 'unevenness'[14] of Strauss's score – is propounded by Sir Georg Solti, who recently suggested that in this opera we may have the rare instance of a masterwork in which the libretto is better than the music.[15] So forthright an opinion is salutary and corrective. It has the effect, since the merits of the music are not seriously in question, of restoring that balance between 'words' and 'music' so appropriate to the spirit of this collaboration, which is increasingly reflected in modern criticism.

Over the course of the years, within the broader perspective of changing critical environment, individual commentators have been unable to agree on the merit either of the music or of the text, or upon the artistic validity of the whole work. Fluctuations of opinion have been wide, and not easy to account for. The 1969 Viennese revival, for instance, even in respect of identical performances, provoked widely conflicting views. Gerhardt Brunner in the Viennese *Illustrierte Kronen Zeitung* wrote:

It was also 'plain cooking' that was on offer at the commencement of the festivities: Richard Strauss's *Arabella* in a revision of the ten-year-old Hans Hotter production. It is doubtful whether there was any pressing need for such a venture. I would go one step further and suggest that it is now high time to separate the wheat from the chaff as far as the repertoire is concerned: and *Arabella* belongs to the latter.[16]

His colleague of *Die Presse* commented:

A relationship to *Rosenkavalier* and some *Fledermaus* echoes in Act 2 have resulted in *Arabella* being designated a derivatory work. This is, however, very far from the truth, because it has, within the bounds of Strauss's musical vocabulary, an atmosphere and a distinctive personal image all of its own. In order to be able to appreciate this, one only needs to listen carefully to the music which characterises Arabella and Mandryka. Such passages bear witness that this lyrical comedy is indeed a masterpiece of musical theatre (thanks also to Hofmannsthal's text!), and represents a heightening of that melodic and conversational technique that Strauss had, before this, handled in a somewhat routine manner. Its melodic beauty is most to be treasured, genuinely 'moving' lyric inspiration linked to a whole world of harmonic feeling that marvellously recreates the impression of the great love ideal.[17]

These extremes of opinion are no doubt rooted in personality and temperament. This apart, since the nature of the work cannot change, one must seek the answer elsewhere. This was not the first time that one branch of critical opinion found itself transforming the ephemeral inadequacies of performance into a value judgement on the work itself. By all accounts, the revival of that gorgeous, now Vienna-domiciled Salzburg production of 1958, without its original cast, left much to be desired.

Indeed, this opera has never fared well as a repertoire piece. Lisa Della Casa's spectacular Viennese debut as Arabella in 1952 had earlier sparked off wide recognition of the merits of a work whose impact is crucially dependent for its success upon the portrayal of its title role. This, by which the whole performance stands or falls, calls for exceptional vocal and characterisatory powers, outstanding acting ability and rare physical charm. Graduation to this challenging role, around which the planning of every new staging of the work must inevitably revolve, represents a significant landmark in a singer's career. This is proved by the large number of festival *Arabella* 'spectaculars' which have been mounted in the last twenty years. But the mystique surrounding such 'celebrity' performances conceals inherent danger. Once the glamour of the initial production has worn off and the stars have departed, diminishing performance impact has, as at least one of the above reports demonstrates, been laid at the door of the work itself. *Arabella* is not a repertoire piece in the accepted sense. Its subtleties demand sustained preparation and constant watchful nursing – operatic 'routine' has proved more than any other factor to be a bar to the steadily growing realisation of its status as a masterwork.

Nonetheless the exceptional qualities of the opera are at last being recognised. Indeed, a review survey from 1933 onwards shows an increasing 'professional' acceptance of the artistic and intellectual claims of a work which has always appealed to the public. The late Dr Willi Schuh, though aware of its weaknesses, esteemed *Arabella* highly, and was one of the first to place it securely in the context of the rest of Strauss's *œuvre*:

Everything is woven together with such refinement and delicacy, fashioned with such enigmatic lightness of spirit, and imbued with such dramatic effectiveness, that one can only speak of Hofmannsthal's *Arabella* as the best comedy for music since *Der Rosenkavalier*. Of course, neither Arabella nor Zdenka, Mandryka or Waldner approaches the heights of a Marschallin, an Octavian, or an Ochs von Lerchenau, and certainly the action is not so original, poetic and sublime as in *Rosenkavalier*, but the simple straightforward libretto comes much closer in spirit to the uncomplicated thoughts of the composer – never had Hofmannsthal adjusted so clearly and so directly to the needs of his partner as here. . .Once more firing the imagination of the composer, the poet allowed the very specific atmosphere generated by the idea to resonate with great sensitivity through his verse. . .*Arabella* is no new Strauss in the way that *Falstaff* was new Verdi, but rather a regeneration, a rejuvenation. . .The music flows from a full heart, it is his warmest since *Rosenkavalier*, and the most delicately conceived since *Ariadne*.[18]

Schuh puts his finger on those features which establish the work as a successful and uniquely legitimate (rather than spectacularly dramatic) expression of music theatre:

In this lyrical comedy, the balance between singing voice and orchestra, the interweaving of the supple conversational and expressive *Arioso* styles, demonstrates that Strauss had achieved heights which even he had never before surpassed. A stylistic synthesis has grown out of the *Rosenkavalier*, *Ariadne* and *Intermezzo* experience, whose combination of full orchestral richness and chamber music delicacy determines the character of the work as a whole. Here, Hofmannsthal and Strauss make relatively little use of ensemble numbers but by placing the main emphasis on the solo voice, they throw the vocal duets into greater relief, enhancing their effect at the most important dramatic moments. . .A marvellous spring of glorious sound, of true musical sensitivity, wells up in this youth-fresh work of Strauss's old age. The mastery which reveals itself in the relationship between voices and orchestra, in the subtly delicate mixture of conversation and broadly flowing lyricism, comes close to the miraculous.[19]

Of course, one should not ignore the enthusiasm of audiences and critics carried away by the great emotional moments of the drama. These have an important part to play: in grand opera, such 'set pieces' would be everything. *Arabella*, however, is no grand opera. The uniqueness of Strauss's approach lies, as Schuh implies, in the grades of transition from a 'sprung', lyrically aware, allusive conversational dialogue, to the melodic highlights represented by duet and *scena* and aria – all of which require, in performance, a most perceptive and sympathetic handling of the score.

Of modern executants, Solti has recognised *Arabella*'s peculiar vulnerability, and has been a major influence in re-establishing its global reputation. William Mann, who interviewed him in 1984 for *Opera*, comments that 'In Frankfurt, Solti added *Arabella* to his Strauss repertory. That was in the 1953/4 season, when *Opera* reported great praise for his vivid, polished advocacy of a piece dubiously regarded by informed (by which I mean "ignorant") operatic taste.' He goes on to relate how, as a young man, Solti was advised by

Strauss himself to 'Read Hofmannsthal's text aloud, at conversational pace and in good German. The spoken tempo in Hofmannsthal's text is the tempo of my music in *Der Rosenkavalier* and in all our operas created together.'[20]

This precept the conductor put into practice in his Vienna recording of 1957 – a performance which takes full acount of the opera's textures and which, by keeping the broad lines of the set pieces moving, yet without sacrificing their lyrical effect or sensuality, integrates them naturally into the subtle dialogue context of the work as a whole. Philip Hope-Wallace, reviewing this particular recording, hails *Arabella* as 'One of the most "atmospherically" attractive operas in the repertory', going on to refer to 'this lovely, glowing recording which should set the seal on its success'. 'Solti's handling of a score which is a mass of fleeting and subtle allusions', he continues, 'is the reverse of pedantic; and when the floodgates need opening he does not hold back. . .A complex and fascinating score.'[21] Five years later, Edward Greenfield talks of his 'admiration for Solti's fine positive qualities. . .a fresh direct approach. . .though he determinedly avoids all sentimentality in the big lyric moments, the freshness of the emotion is vividly conveyed'.[22]

Thus, in recent years the critical climate has perceptibly eased. The work still has its detractors and some reservations, very properly, still exist over musical and dramatic weaknesses in the score. The modern view is, one feels, however, far removed from that of Olin Downes' – a final echo of pre-war attitudes following the American premiere of 1955, which speaks of an opera

singularly devoid of genuine musical invention, genuine characterisation or very much of anything that carries conviction or sincerity to the listener. That it is a workmanlike job, in the setting of a singularly bad libretto, goes without saying. But what could Strauss, or any dramatic composer, reasonably have expected to do with this shoddy material? At the best he is plausible, gay in the ballroom scene and, in short stretches, genuinely sentimental. The opera is prevailingly dull, uninspired, unoriginal.[23]

Downes makes the commonplace comparison with *Rosenkavalier*, which Norman Del Mar refreshingly dismisses:

Despite more regular revivals than any of Strauss' later operas, it has taken *Arabella* all too long to shake itself clear of that damaging comparison. For when it comes to the point, of far greater importance is its own particular quality of warmth and glowing beauty. Even the orchestration has a timbre unique amongst Strauss' operas up to this time, and it is interesting that with masterly restraint Strauss uses no percussion throughout the work other than timpani. Fortunately in recent years the opera has begun to occupy a position of popular prestige in its own right as a heart-searching character study clothed in gay and attractive comedy, despite some far-fetched situations and occasional weak moments, especially in the latter part of the second act.[24]

This view is reinforced by Michael Kennedy in an illuminating report of the 1984 Glyndebourne production of the opera:

If any impressions still lingered that *Arabella*, the last Strauss–Hofmannsthal collaboration, was a poor relation of their *Rosenkavalier*, it was emphatically and finally dispelled at Glyndebourne on Saturday. The opera is a year older than the festival, but this was its first production there and as had been expected, it found its ideal setting in this house. John Cox's marvellous production not only crowns his Strauss cycle but it is one of the finest one could hope to encounter. The Glyndebourne touch with Strauss has again worked enchantment. Julia Trevelyan Oman's sets, carefully researched, bring the Vienna of 1860 to life in hotel and ballroom with an authenticity that extends to such detail as the splendid device for holding a broadsheet newspaper. The heroine's dresses are as true to period and class as are those of the cabbies' ball mascot, the Fiakermilli. The strength of Mr. Cox's production lies in the motivation he gives to the smallest roles equally with the principals. A plot that can seem artificial becomes credible and touching. The notoriously intractable end of Act 2 and start of Act 3 was brilliantly handled. I had never thought to be convinced by Fiakermilli (Eileen Hulse), but I was. On a par in uncovering layers of often overlooked detail in one of Strauss' most bejewelled scores was Bernard Haitink's interpretation. The meeting between the wealthy and naïve Mandryka and Arabella's impoverished father sparkled like a symphonic scherzo and in the love duet and final scene the playing of the London Philharmonic Orchestra had all the indispensable richness and warmth. Arabella was portrayed with impassioned and lyrical grace by the American soprano Ashley Putnam, her vocal splendour enhanced by sympathetic and intelligent insights into this girl's complex character. Her triumph was shared by the Dutch baritone John Bröcheler's Mandryka in a notable British debut which restored elegant legato singing to a role that sometimes can sound like one long staccato bark. Gianna Rolandi's vulnerable Zdenka, Artur Korn's Waldner (treated as no buffoon), Regina Sarfaty's actressy Adelaide and Keith Lewis's Matteo headed the secondary roles.[25]

Kennedy's account confirms, by implication, the critical reassessment that we have seen developing over the years. The significance of this production, happily captured for posterity on film, can be found in those interpretative refinements, appropriate to the smaller opera house, which in their embodiment of the Strauss/Hofmannsthal concept of musical theatre would surely have delighted the collaborators. Strauss's ability to mirror the emotional subtlety of conversational dialogue is implicit in that ideal realisation of intimate theatre which, strengthened by his chamber music style, is prompted by the characteristic rhythmic subtlety of Hofmannsthal's text. As demonstrated at Glyndebourne, the utmost precision of on-stage production detail is initiated by the natural flexibility of Hofmannsthal's lines, which are so sensitively recreated in Strauss' *parlando* manner. We have here to do with a stage work which achieves expressive impact by holding the essential elements of word, music and action in balance – lyricism and musical feeling is everywhere, but 'music' never intrudes unless by conscious intent. It is, on the other hand, legitimately exploited; raised to pre-eminence as the supreme emotional vehicle by the expressive and interpretational needs of the action and the drama. It is the underlying lyricism which runs through Hofmannsthal's verse, so superbly defined and exploited by the composer, which lends that uniqueness and dramatic integrity to their joint achievement in *Arabella*: a landmark in the history of twentieth-century conversational opera.

Arabella is successful because it transfers the subtlety of the spoken play directly and effectively to the operatic stage. This achievement is the result of a high degree of collaborative understanding between Strauss and Hofmannsthal in the years preceding the latter's sudden death. The process started with *Der Rosenkavalier* and continued through *Ariadne*, the first version of which, juxtaposing both play and opera, met with limited success. These works, together with Hofmannsthal's Viennese comedies of the early 1920s, are indicative of a thrust towards the integration of lyric drama and the musical stage. Experience had already proved that such a synthesis was best approached from the more relaxed standpoint of operatic comedy. In the case of *Arabella* the impetus for a return to this *genre* came from Strauss, but one already recognises in Hofmannsthal's wonted alternation – even harnessing – of serious and comic projects an eagerness, after *Helena* and *Der Turm*, to tap once more a lighter theatrical vein. The style of the new opera was never in doubt, being broadly conceived in the spirit of *Der Rosenkavalier*, whose libretto Reinhardt had once pronounced worthy of stage performance in its own right.[1] To dismiss *Arabella* as an imitation of the earlier *Comedy for Music*, however – a trap into which many writers have fallen – simply will not do. The published correspondence, indeed, stimulates analogy, but both Hofmannsthal and Strauss, while acknowledging privately a common source and inspiration, were fully aware of the stylistic distance travelled in the sixteen or so years which separated the composition of the two works. As reviews and critiques have shown, comparisons are inevitable, but resemblances, far from being imitative, exemplify, rather, Hofmannsthal's theatrical integrity, which consistently, throughout his *œuvre*, employs recurring ideas, situations, topics and character-types.

There are, indeed, certain parallels to be drawn between *Rosenkavalier* and *Arabella*, the most obvious stemming from their common Viennese setting and a *wienerisch*-ness directly stimulated by Hofmannsthal's use of dialect. Dramatically speaking, too, both works revolve around the 'lover's encounter', envisaged by Hofmannsthal as a moment of soul recognition 'by which the stars are moved',[2] whose fulfilment is mutually experienced in the traditional 'happy ending'. By their utilisation of dramatic disguises, misunderstandings, suspicions and jealousies, both operas may be designated 'comedies of intrigue', while in each case the central theme, the coming together of the lovers, involves a revival of family fortunes or the realisation of dynastic hopes. Another device common to each – the 'breeches' role – is reminiscent of Mozart's *Figaro*, although the analogy is more appropriate to *Rosenkavalier*, owing to its period setting and to the provenance of the Octavian concept. On the other hand, the arrival of a character (Ochs, Mandryka) from the provinces injects into each of the operas a 'foreign' element which, basically Austrian though not specifically Viennese, serves to intensify the action, prompting a degree of social contrast in terms of manners, behaviour, ideals and etiquette. Furthermore, a correspondence of theatrical devices – girl/boy disguises, overheard conversations and bedroom incidents – demonstrates a mechanical as well as a spatial effectiveness of set and situation, which all nevertheless stems directly from the poet's acknowledged baroque models.

Considered in this context the above correlations appear less formidable and certainly less significant. The dubious Vienna of *Arabella*, for instance, is, by virtue of its contemporariness, historically more realistic – less mythical – than the courtly world of its predecessor. Furthermore, the straightforward 'girl as boy' Zdenka/Zdenko disguise is simpler in concept than the 'girl as boy as girl' Octavian/Mirandel rôle – each opera, of course, taking as its starting point a different sexual premise. The intrigue surrounding the *Rosenkavalier* disguises has, indeed, a certain irresponsible 'masqueradelike' quality even when, with Sophie's future at stake, things are at their most serious. In *Arabella*, however, the game is played out in deadly earnest on all sides; Arabella's marriage will have a decisive impact upon the family fortunes, and Zdenka, too, plays her hand 'for real' – the bedroom assignation with Matteo represents a last desperate wager against seemingly insuperable odds. Finally, the apparent resemblance between Ochs and Mandryka also, in the last resort, proves superficial. Ochs's breeding, despite a certain *sang-froid*, is coarse and somewhat threadbare: the high-minded renunciation of the Marschallin, for instance, is quite foreign to his nature.

Mandryka, with less in the way of pedigree, shows himself more genuinely noble; his sensitivity and corresponding vulnerability appear quite out of keeping with Ochs's self-opinionated blusterings. It is just this vulnerability which arouses audience sympathy on his behalf; his honesty and 'provincial' integrity set him above the fashionable Viennese circles in which he is forced to move, while his wealth and foreignness grant him an attractive and mysterious notoriety.

It is, of course, ultimately from the text that the music springs; and one inevitably turns to the literary concept – to the libretto – for interpretative clues. One should, however, guard against too symbolistic a reading of *Arabella* – despite an innate allusiveness that relates to manners, morals, and society. Hofmannsthal himself confirms this when he talks of the possible emergence of 'something of a picture of social history' in the work.[3] His interest in rank, status and background, however, was primarily a means of delineating character and fuelling dramatic motivation; he never tired of exploring the psychological tensions inherent in the stringent Viennese class barriers. The formal, strictly regulated eighteenth-century court *milieu* of *Der Rosenkavalier* gives way in *Der Schwierige* and *Arabella* to eras where social unrest was only just below the surface, where class distinction, owing to Austrian Imperial decline, was far less clear-cut. This, a crucial formative period in Hofmannsthal's own life, had initiated a twentieth-century world which discarded former values; a phenomenon with which, in common with his contemporaries, he needed to come to terms. The Hofmannsthal who could so completely master the niceties of Theresian court and society etiquette is, of course, perfectly at home in the pre-1914–18 war world of *Der Schwierige*, with whose hero, Hans Karl Bühl, he is easily identifiable. In *Arabella*, there is no directly identifiable autobiographical element of this nature.

The atmosphere of decay, represented by Waldner's gambling morals, is portrayed against the vulnerable affluence of Imperial Vienna. Such precarious living epitomises the broader social context in which the Waldners move. Historically speaking this is also hollow, a sham; a world which had already sowed the seeds of its own destruction. Hofmannsthal uses this concept to motivate the drama, contrasting the stolid splendour of a Viennese inner-city hotel with the poverty-stricken expired gentility of its clients, while Adelaide's neurotic fantasies vie with Arabella's pessimistic acceptance of her matrimonial fate; Zdenka's conspiratorial naïvety is sharply set off by her sister's candid, open nature, while from the backwoods of a far-flung empire Mandryka picks his way, with peasant-like honesty but not without aplomb, through the maze of high-society city slickness. The *Fiakerball*, traditionally the great social leveller, combines all these elements, juxtaposing aristocrat and commoner, rich and poor, the sophisticate and the provincial. It is not only an effective symbol of the social maelstrom of the era but also a potent dramatic concept, proposing a backcloth against which the central characters are projected. Thus its ceremonial glitter throws Mandryka's gaucheness into relief at the beginning of Act 2, while the all-pervading sophistication of the waltz lends sharper focus to his honest countryman's sincerity during the courtship scene. In the act's *finale* his outrageous behaviour signals a general dissipation which even offends the socially questionable Waldner parents. Such a framework well suits Hofmannsthal's dramatic purpose – it is a situation where all is in a state of flux: where anything can happen.

Similar dualities characterise the language of the opera, where, despite the late-nineteenth-century disintegration of social barriers, class differences are still carefully measured and the speech patterns of Kaiser Franz Josef's Vienna securely drawn. Thus, during Adelaide's conversation with the Fortune-teller, the latter's typically Viennese 'Euer Gnaden' reassuringly acknowledges the former's nobility. Adelaide veers between domestic familiarity (to Waldner) and aristocratic pride exemplified by her justly arrogant treatment of Mandryka at the end of Act 2. The generation gap, subtly maintained by archaisms handed down from an earlier courtly tradition, is manifest in a smattering of gallicisms such as Adelaide's 'O Wien! Die Stadt der Médisance' or Waldner's 'Jetzt habe ich mein richtiges Vis-à-Vis'. The latter, however, not often on his dignity, exudes for the most part a *wienerisch* geniality which, spilling over into his speech, neatly characterises the *gemütlich* card-playing low life with which he identifies. The Austrian Hofmannsthal is indeed fortunate heir to a rich dialectal tradition upon which he draws freely, providing as one of his chiefest delights linguistic characterisations, extending with absolute consistency down to the minutest textual detail. Such phrases as 'So ist ein Mädel' and 'Ich bleib ein Bub' confirm Zdenka's Austrianness as clearly as 'Gospodar' and 'Teschek' provide the clue to Mandryka's Slavonic (Croatian) origins. His use of Viennese patois, 'Er ist ein biss'l blutig geworden' or 'Milli, gib mir ein Bußl', is entirely consistent with a cultural bureaucracy reaching to the furthest outposts of the empire. It is from this not so alien world that Mandryka comes, bringing with him a touching provincial reverence for the *Kaiserstadt*; he is not so much a visitor to a foreign capital as a countryman in town, with all the conflict of attitudes and values that that implies.

A further refinement of language, one with both personal and social implications, is to be found in the use of the intimate 'du' form. The distinction in address between 'du' and 'Sie', specifically defining the nature and closeness of relationships, has a significance which the English-speaking listener is apt to overlook. In Act 2, during the courtship scene, the 'du' is introduced, appropriately enough, at Mandryka's account of the village betrothal ritual. As yet, Arabella retains the somewhat rhetorical 'Sie', but both revert to the intimate form at the duet, 'Und du wirst mein Gebieter sein'. At once, Arabella's 'Jetzt aber fahren Sie nach Haus' restores the mood of polite formality, marking the end of an intimate episode, and a return to the 'real' world of social convention which surrounds them. The 'du' form is eventually exploited to chart the emotional temperature between the lovers in Act 3; whereas earlier, in the Matteo/Arabella exchanges, it also has a particularly telling, almost comic, even poignant role to play.

All these various ideas, forms and expressions were employed by Hofmannsthal to motivate the drama, define the characters and establish the atmosphere of the work. In addition, they each contribute to a broader interpretative concept which, on the poet's own admission, highlights, against a mundane custom-ridden background, the unconventional girl he conceives Arabella to be. She appears in rounder dimension than her prototype, Crescence, in *Der Schwierige* – a woman who also shapes her own destiny; as Hofmannsthal himself asserted, Arabella is 'conscious of her strength and of the hazards she runs, completely mistress of the situation. . . an entirely modern character'.[4] She also has a dual function; representative of the decaying order from which she has sprung, her idealistic longings are symbolised by her love for Mandryka. An unquestioned integrity enables her to transcend her upbringing, encouraging her to envisage and to seek out this new spiritual goal.

It is this aspiration, this dream of the immutability of love permeating both *Arabella* and *Rosenkavalier*, that confirms Hofmannsthal's underlying and irrepressible romanticism. Indeed, the Sophie/Octavian and Arabella/Mandryka relationships, dependent upon the validity of the *ewige Liebe* concept, have inescapable Wagnerian overtones. The collaborators were acutely aware, in the wake of post-Wagnerian critical rumblings over the 'sleep' potions in *Helena*, of the connotations of Arabella's symbolic 'glass of water'. These had, at the time, been discounted by Hofmannsthal ('after all, Wagner did not, for heaven's sake, *invent* these potions!'[5]), who, after Strauss's current warning ('the joke – "Hofmannsthal must have got water on the brain" – is too cheap to be passed over by a single witty journalist'[6]), replied, 'I can't see for the life of me why the magic potions in *Helena* should now prevent me from introducing the presentation of so much as a glass of water [in *Arabella*].'[7] Whereas the *Tristan* potions emphasise at the outset a passion which fuels and motivates the drama, in *Arabella* the 'glass of water' symbolises that ultimate union which confirms its happy outcome. The distance between these concepts is clear; on the one hand the symbolic drink opens up a world of guilt and emotional torment ending in disastrous ecstasy – on the other it speaks eternal, living commitment, confirming the rightness ('der Richtige') of Arabella's choice: it is the advent of Mandryka, against all the odds, that is significant in *Arabella* – his existence holds out real hope for the fulfilment of her dreams.

In the broader sense, Mandryka's suspicions (Acts 2 and 3) are, although in the event understandable, unworthy of him, demonstrating how much he still has to learn about Arabella's true nature. She will not plight her troth lightly, and once committed, once her love is given, she will never draw back. It is this discovery, the chief burden of Act 3, which, by testing the strength of their attachment, occupies a vital place in the dramatic scheme of the work. This is the truth that Mandryka, as the recipient of a forgiveness of which he admits himself to be unworthy, finally recognises. In turn, Arabella, forced to withstand unjust accusations which threaten the dissolution of her dearest hopes and dreams, yet appreciates the 'loss of face' attendant upon Mandryka's acknowledgement of error – the more difficult for him since his recantation has necessarily to be public. This is an important enabling factor in her exercise of forgiveness. Her sacrifice is the greater because her hurt, by virtue of its unjustness, is the keener, but ultimately the sacrifice has to be, and is, mutual. It is the nobility of repentance, understanding and forgiveness that finally brings the lovers together.

Such nobility also appertains to Zdenka. As Arabella points out,[8] it is ultimately from her and by her example that the greater lesson of love is learned. Prepared to hazard everything for Matteo and Arabella, her desperate self-giving is a grave social risk – particularly when discovered – it is an act of nobility and sacrifice, and is recognised as such by all parties concerned. The Act 3 *dénouement*, therefore, transforms what might have been regarded as sordid, cynical or a dangerous loss of caste into something truly selfless and noble. In real terms, of course, the Zdenka/Matteo assignation is quite as untenable as Matteo's sudden switch of affection from the older to the younger sister. It is, however, a venerable theatrical device, gesturing, like *Rosenkavalier*, towards the darkened pavilions of *Figaro*; tactics which, 'suspending disbelief', crave and win acceptance from an indulgent audience.

Mandryka remains a figure of considerable power, depth and interest. Like Arabella, this is a particularly strong role, offering superb opportunities to the accomplished artist. Although, by virtue of its length and predominantly high tessitura, fearsomely difficult, it lends itself, as does that of Arabella, to powerful impersonation by an outstanding actor-singer. Alfred Jerger in the 1930s established his reputation with the part, and amongst modern executants Fischer-Dieskau, with his aristocratic grace and handsomeness, seemed as ideally suited to its performance as did the strikingly lovely Della Casa as Arabella with her uncanny stage presence. Impulsive, yet at the same time profoundly serious, Mandryka is capable of terrible rage and of wild extravagance. Exuding a primitive strength, he is also naïve and childlike, but at all times master of himself. His dignity and obvious integrity, characteristic of the old Empire which he represents, stand in refreshing contrast to the unstable social environment which he has entered. There, however, he will not remain, but will return to the real world of his forests and villages. Since he takes Arabella with him, he also imbues the provincial environment with a breath of that sophistication, elegance and charm so characteristic of the Viennese spirit. Such a fortuitous and genealogically healthy mingling of fortune and blood points the way to a promising and hopeful future.[9]

As far as Strauss was concerned, however, *Arabella*'s appeal was purely on grounds of human interest and practicality. Hofmannsthal refrained from involving him in any form of metaphysical discussion, restricting his comments purely to psychological and dramatic affairs. Psychological motivation was as important to Strauss as was the technical challenge presented by the text, with its carefully controlled rhythmic patterns, conversational pace and poetic conception. These were qualities to which Strauss could respond and in which he revelled. In the execution of the down-to-earth technical function he became, from time to time, critical of areas where Hofmannsthal, overcome by esoteric considerations, had run roughshod over the principles of sound dramatic construction. The textual density of Hofmannsthal's libretto presented Strauss with no problem at all. As closely worked and as subtly motivated as any spoken play, it provided the composer with the opportunity to create that brand of conversational realism for which he had, musically, technically equipped himself and which enabled him to leap over his 'German 19th century shadow'[10] to find a path around the Wagnerian mountain.[11]

Herein, nevertheless, lies one of the problems which beset non-German-speaking audiences. In Hofmannsthal's work, the motivational detail depends, particularly for its finer interpretative effects, upon an unprecedented linguistic subtlety. While Strauss was adept and resourceful in his 'pointing' of such passages, the need to cover the textual ground quickly, resulting in a dialogue pace and manner of delivery, can, for the non-linguist, lead to a breakdown of comprehensibility. All too often for such audiences the remedy employed has been indiscriminate cutting of the score, a misconceived attempt to relieve the 'boredom' of what are unjustly described as 'arid' passages, at the cost of damage to the overall structure of the work. Such excisions, already noted in the final act of *Arabella*, are impossible to justify. So meticulous is Hofmannsthal's motivic thought process that nothing can be omitted without distorting the dramatic concept; so complementary are text and music that such treatment not only interrupts the logical development of the action, but also damages the musical structure, negating the entire musico-dramatic effect.

This is certainly one of the chief reasons why English and American critics were slow to grant *Arabella* the acclaim it deserved, and, as we have seen, the effect of earlier adverse opinion lingers in some quarters even today. Reservations have also been expressed about the supposedly looser dramatic construction of the two final acts, as well as of the admittedly far-fetched outcome of the Zdenka/Matteo assignation of Act 3. Perhaps something might have been done about the somewhat derivative nature of the Act 2 *finale*, had Hofmannsthal lived.[12] The last act, as we have seen, is all too often distorted in performance by cuts which invariably include the beautiful Arabella/Zdenka exchanges from Fig. 110 to Fig. 119[6]. Here, the sisters' consolatory confidences are psychologically all-important; diverting Arabella's attention from the guilt-ridden Mandryka, they place the outcome of forgiveness in doubt, adding poignancy and significance to reiterations of the phrase 'Was jetzt noch kommt!' This whole passage, a dramatic *tour de force*, is superbly handled by Hofmannsthal and Strauss, culminating in a powerful structural and emotional climax at 'Brautwerbung kommt!' – its omission, in performance, is quite indefensible. As far as the intimacies between Zdenka and Matteo are concerned, one can only point out that this is, after all, opera. Sometimes disbelief has to be suspended, and Strauss at least redeems the situation both here and later in the act by supplying music of extraordinary freshness and charm.

William Mann is on the right lines when he wisely comments, 'It is perfectly possible to find weaknesses or shortcomings in *Arabella*, and still to find it an enchanting and inspiring opera.'[13] One can only endorse this view. It is hardly important if *Arabella* falls short of ultimate perfection. It is with the work's positive qualities, with what has been accomplished, that we should concern ourselves – and that is much. One can point to a chamber-music sensitivity of orchestration, granting a vocal intelligibility which enables the text to stand in equal partnership with the music. One can admire the supple expressivity of a melodic line which mirrors verbal inflection; which demonstrates a complementary rhythmic and musical control capable of those 'transitions from dialogue into the lyrical mood'[14] which dictate the dramatic pace of the work and reflect the subtlety of Hofmannsthal's achievement. In addition, one recognises an overall constructional integrity springing from the musical and dramatic motivic coherence that underpins this opera – the direct result of a close and long-standing collaborative experience. Ultimately, however, the overall impression of the work's profoundly human and theatrical qualities remains. Such a concept, with its congenial Viennese *milieu*, its wide range of picturesque characters, and charming heroine, could not but appeal to Strauss. It held out its own particular challenge – calling for a refinement of technique the achievement of which is the measure of his success. Mann talks of 'the uncluttered straightforwardness of the poetic diction, the perfectly judged weight and tunefulness'[15] of the *Arabella* music. These were the qualities for which Strauss and Hofmannsthal were aiming in *Arabella*; their achievement was the creation of a new *genre* of music theatre – a fitting tribute to this unique artistic collaboration.

Appendix 1   An additional quartet

The following ensemble was written at Strauss's instigation. It was to have been inserted after Waldner's declaration to Arabella, Adelaide and Zdenka of Mandryka's suit (after Mandryka's exit following his interview with Waldner), and was to precede the final 'letter' scene of the original (revised) version – see p. 53. Strauss had, in the first instance, asked for a quintet – presumably to include Mandryka – but Hofmannsthal obviously preferred not to anticipate the important second-act meeting between the lovers. It would, indeed, have been illogical to include Mandryka in the ensemble, especially if the last scene of the act was still to revolve around Arabella's letter accepting the building contractor's marriage offer. In the event one concludes that Strauss was right to omit the quartet – as it stands, it hardly furthers the action; its essence (Arabella's perplexity and doubt about her future) was in due course more effectively incorporated into the *Mein Elemer* finale. See Strauss/Hofmannsthal, *Correspondence*, letters of 6 May 1928, 9 May 1928 and 21 June 1928, pp. 475–81. The *Quartet* text is quoted in Hugo von Hofmannsthal, *Gesammelte Werke, Lustspiele 4*, ed. H. Steiner (Fischer, Frankfurt, 1956), pp. 470–1, and also in Hugo von Hofmannsthal, *Sämtliche Werke*, vol. 26, *Operndichtungen 4*, ed. Hans Albrecht Koch (Fischer, Frankfurt, 1976), pp. 95–6.

> ADELAIDE (*tenderly*)
> Be quiet, hide your good fortune, confide in me alone,
> the envy of the wicked world is boundless! –
> only with your mother who has schemed and hoped for it,
> must the secret of your new-won happiness be shared;
> the words of the prophetess will come true,
> the stars will have it so,
> and your sore tried afflicted mother blesses you!

136

ADELAIDE (*zärtlich*)
Schweig still, verbirg dein Glück, verbirgs bei mir,
der Neid der bösen Welt ist ohne Grenzen!
bei deiner Mutter, die dirs aufgebaut,
verbirg dein junges Glück;
die Worte der Prophetin werden Wahrheit,
die Sterne wollen es,
und deine leidgeprüfte Mutter segnet dich!

WALDNER (*together with her*)
From one day to another all has changed completely
Long the cards have mocked me, so long has fortune frowned,
suddenly she smiles! All doors are opened!
A magic voice rings out: 'Help yourself, help yourself!'
and the beggar changes into a king again!

WALDNER (*zugleich mit ihr*)
Von einem Tag zum andern ändert sich gar viel!
Lang sind die Karten bös, und finster schaut das Glück,
auf einmal lächeln sie, und alle Türen gehen auf!
Ein Zauberwort ertönt: Bediene dich, bediene dich!
und aus dem Bettler wird ein König wiederum!

ZDENKA (*with folded hands together with the other two*)
O God in Heaven, bring her happiness
and somewhere, unnoticed, let me die in peace!
This the prophetess saw, this she foretold,
she radiant in light - and I plunged into darkness.
She is so dear and beautiful, I take my leave
and even as I go, I bless you, Oh my sister!

ZDENKA (*mit gefalteten Händen zugleich mit ihnen beiden*)
O Gott im Himmel, laß sie glücklich werden
und mich laß sterben in der Stille irgendwo!
So hat ja die Prophetin es gesehn,
sie ganz im Licht und ich hinab ins Dunkel.
Sie ist so schön und lieb, ich werde gehen
und noch im Gehen werd ich dich segnen, meine Schwester!

ARABELLA (*together with the others, only the last line alone*)
O God, they are all so pleased, everyone is smiling -
they are all happy, heavy my heart alone!
So readily they trust to luck, yet ever and again
comes disappointment. Bitter tears
rain in my heart, falling continually,
a heart which should be full of sweentess and of joy!
O God, let this illusion quickly pass -
for illusion it will be, illusion only
I feel it coming!

ARABELLA (*zugleich mit ihnen allen, nur die letzte Zeile allein*)
O Gott, sie freuen sich, sie lächeln alle –
so leichte Herzen haben sie, und nur mein Herz ist schwer!
so schnell vertrauen sie aufs Glück, und immer wieder
kommt die Enttäuschung, und ein bitterer Tropfen
fällt in mein Herz und wiederum ein Tropfen –
und süß und freudig soll ein Herz doch sein!
O Gott, laß diese neue Täuschung schnell vorübergehn –
denn es wird Täuschung und nur Täuschung sein,
ich fühls voraus!

Appendix 2　The recordings

Of the available recordings of *Arabella* the Solti/Decca set still holds its place despite competition from the very recent Tate/Decca issue. These two are the only recordings that present the work complete without cuts of any description. Although the Tate discs with Kiri Te Kanawa have much to recommend them, particularly in quality of sound, the overall style and manner of performance cannot be compared with the earlier Vienna issue, which is, for all its years, still respectable as sound, and has an experienced cast headed by Della Casa at the height of her powers.

Other available discs all suffer from cuts, the Sawallisch/EMI only minimally so, but here, although those which mar the Keilberth/DGG set (particularly in Act 3) are avoided, the recorded balance between voice and orchestra is uncomfortable. The Rennert is a pirated disc and has serious technical flaws, especially in Act 2. The Böhm historical issue has a delightful Zdenka (the young Della Casa), and Gueden's perceptive and experienced Arabella as well as Hotter's majestic Mandryka. It creates a valuable link between the modern performing tradition and that of Strauss's time and one particularly admires Böhm's objective pacing of the performance. Keilberth and Tate both err in this respect with a tendency to indulge in the sort of tempo exaggerations that Strauss himself resolutely fought against in the interpretation of his works.

For the Haitink/Glyndebourne filmed performance, despite regrettable Act 3 cuts (almost exactly in line with Keilberth), a special case must be made for the unique visual impact of John Cox's stylish production of 1984.

The cuts employed in the complete recordings are detailed below: numbers in larger type refer to the rehearsal figures of the full score; numbers in smaller type indicate the bar numbers computed from these figures.

139

Böhm/Salzburg

Act 1: −. Act 2: 105^9–106, 120–121, 130–132, 148–end. Acts 2 & 3 combined. Act 3: 103–104, 109–114^{14}

Solti/Vienna

Act 1: −. Act 2: −. Act 3: −

Keilberth/Munich

Act 1: −. Act 2: 120–121, 128–132, 148–end. Acts 2 & 3 combined. Act 3: 36–41, 65^{10}–69, 86–90, 103–104, 110^7–119^5

Rennert/Rome

Act 1: −. Act 2: −. Act 3: 36–41, 65^{10}–69, 75–77, 103–104, 110^7–119^5

Sawallisch/Munich

Act 1: −. Act 2: −. Act 3: 103–104. Acts 2 & 3 combined

Haitink/Glyndebourne

Act 1: −. Act 2: 128–132. Act 3: 36^1–41, 65^{10}–69, 75–77, 103–104, 110^7–119^5

Tate/Covent Garden

Act 1: −. Act 2: −. Act 3: −

Notes

1 Strauss and Hofmannsthal: the collaborative background

1 *Correspondence*, 7 March 1906 (H), pp. 2–3
2 *Ibid.*, 11 March 1906 (S), p. 3
3 *Ibid.*, p. xx
4 Hugo von Hofmannsthal, *Die Wege und die Begegnungen* (1913), quoted in Brian Keith-Smith, 'Hugo von Hofmannsthal', in *German Men of Letters*, ed. Alex Natan, 2 vols. (Oswald Wolff, London, 1961)
5 Including *Prinz Eugen* (1915), *Maria Theresia* (1917), *Die Idee Europa* (1917) and *Grillparzer* (1922)
6 Hofmannsthal, 'Festspiel in Salzburg', quoted in Keith-Smith, *Hofmannsthal*, p. 267
7 Quoted in Ernst Krause, *Richard Strauss*, trans. John Coombs (Collet's London, 1964), p. 414
8 *Correspondence*, 22 October 1911 (H), p. 104
9 *Ibid.*, 30 January 1912 (H), p. 116
10 *Ibid.*, 23 July 1928 (S), p. 492
11 *Ibid.*, 18 October 1908 (H), p. 26
12 *Ibid.*, 19 July 1911 (S), pp. 95–6
13 Richard Strauss, 'Vorwort zu Intermezzo', in *Betrachtungen und Erinnerungen* (Atlantis, Zurich, 1949), p. 145
14 *Correspondence*, 23 June 1912 (H), p. 133
15 *Ibid.*, 8 November 1924 (H), p. 393
16 *Ibid.*
17 *Ibid.*, 22 September 1923 (S), p. 366
18 Hofmannsthal, *Der Turm* (1924)
19 *Correspondence*, 8 November 1924 (H), p. 394
20 *Ibid.*, 16 July 1929 (S), p. 537

2 Synopsis

1 Hugo von Hofmannsthal, *Arabella*, libretto (Adolph Fürstner, Berlin, 1933), p. 19:

> Aber der Richtige – wenn's einen gibt für mich auf dieser Welt,
> der wird einmal dastehn, da vor mir
> und wird mich anschaun, und ich ihn,
> und keine Zweifel werden sein und keine Fragen,
> und selig werd' ich sein und gehorsam wie ein Kind!

Ich weiß nicht wie du bist, ich weiß nicht, ob du Recht hast –
dazu hab' ich dich viel zu lieb! Ich will nur, daß du glücklich wirst
mit einem der's verdient! und helfen will ich dir dazu.
So hat ja die Prophetin es gesehn,
sie ganz im Licht, und ich hinab ins Dunkel.
Sie ist so schön und so lieb – ich werde gehn,
und noch im Gehn werd' ich dich segnen, meine Schwester.

2 *Ibid.*, p. 34:

Mein sind die Wälder, meine sind die Dörfer.
Viertausend Untertanen beten, daß ich glücklich sei,
und ich, mit aufgehobenen Händen bitte ich:
Herr Vater, geben mir die gnädige Tochter,
geben Sie mir zur Frau, die jetzt seit vierzehn Wochen
jeden Gedanken in dieser Brust regiert.

3 *Ibid.*, p. 41:

Mein Elemer! – das hat so einen sonderbaren Klang. . .
Er mein – ich sein. Was ist denn das,
mir ist ja, wie wenn eine Angst mich überfiele –
und eine Sehnsucht. . .ja, nach was denn auf der Welt.
Nach dem Matteo? Weil er immer sagt,
er kann nicht leben ohne mich und mich so anschaut
mit Augen wie ein Kind?
Nach dem Matteo sehnt sich nichts in mir!
Ich möchte meinen fremden Mann einmal noch sehen!
Ich möchte einmal seine Stimme hören! Seine Stimme.
Dann, dann wär' er wie die anderen für mich. –
Wie sagt die Zdenka: daß wir warten müssen, bis uns einer wählt,
und sonst sind wir verloren.
Verheirat't mit dem Elemer?
Was rührt mich denn so an, als trät' ich einem übers Grab?
Ist das der fremde Mann, mit dem ich nie ein Wort geredet hab',
zieht der im Dunkel so an mir?
Herr Gott, er ist ja sicher ein verheirateter Mann,
und ich soll, und ich werd' ihn nicht mehr wiedersehen!
Und heut und heut ist Faschingsdienstag, und heut abend ist mein
   Ball –
von dem bin ich die Königin und dann. . .

4 *Ibid.*, p. 46:

Ich habe eine Frau gehabt, sehr schön, sehr engelsgut.
Sie ist zwei Jahr nur bei mir geblieben.
Dann hat der Herrgott sie zu sich gerufen schnell.
Zu jung war ich und noch nicht gut genug für solchen Engel.

5 *Ibid.*, p. 47:

So schön sind Sie – eine Gewalt ist in Ihren Zügen,
sich einzudrücken in die Seele wie weiches Wachs!

Über den einfachen Menschen, den Felder und Wälder umgeben,
ist ein solche Gewalt sehr groß, und er wird wie ein Träumer,
wie ein Besessener wird er, und er faßt den Entschluß mit der Seele,
einen ganzen Entschluß, und wie er entschlossen ist, so muß er
handeln!

6 *Ibid.*, pp. 49–50:

So fließt die helle stille Donau mir beim Haus vorbei,
und hat mir dich gebracht! Du Allerschönste! –
Und heute abend noch, zur Schlafenszeit,
wärst du ein Mädchen aus den Dörfen, einem meinigen,
du müßtest mir zum Brunnen gehen hinter deines Vaters Haus
und klares Wasser schöpfen einen Becher voll
und mir ihn reichen vor der Schwelle, daß ich dein Verlobter bin
vor Gott und vor den Menschen, meine Allerschönste!

So wie Sie sind, so hab' ich keinen Menschen je geseh'n!
Sie bringen Ihre eigne Lebensluft mit sich,
und was nicht Ihnen zugehört, das ist nicht da für Sie.

Darum kann ich erst leben, wenn ich etwas Herrliches
erhöhe über mich, und so in dieser Stunde
erhöhe ich dich, und wähle dich zu meiner Frau,
und wo ich Herr bin, wirst du Herrin sein
und wirst gebieten, wo ich der Gebieter bin!

Und du wirst mein Gebieter sein, und ich dir untertan.
Dein Haus wird mein Haus sein,
in deinem Grab will ich mit dir begraben sein –
so gebe ich mich dir auf Zeit und Ewigkeit.

7 *Ibid.*, pp. 51–2:

Die Wiener Herr'n verstehn sich
auf die Astronomie:
die könnten von der Sternwart sein
und wissen gar nicht wie!
Sie finden einen neuen Stern
gar schnell heraus, die Wiener Herr'n,
den machen sie zur Königin
an ihrem Firmament!
Zu der dann schallt es im Verein:
Du sollst unseres Festes Königin sein!

8 *Ibid.*, pp. 67–8:

Ging durch einen Wald, weiß nich durch welchen!
Fand ein Mädchen, weiß nicht, wessen Tochter!
Trat ihr auf den Fuß, weiß nicht auf welchen,
fing es an zu schrei'n, weiß nicht warum doch,
seht den Wicht, wie der sich denkt die Liebe!

Wohl stünd's an, ihm Kanne Wein zu geben,

Wein zu geben, Becher nicht zu geben,
mag der Wicht aus schwerer Kanne trinken,
mag sich plagen bis zu klügeren Tagen!

Wohl stünd's an, mich Mädchen ihm zu geben,
mich zu geben, doch kein Bett zu geben.
Mag der Kerl auf bloßer Erde schlafen,
mag sich plagen bis zu klügeren Tagen!

Für heut fährt sie nach Haus zu ihrem Schlüsselherrn,
von Morgen an ist sie die Meinige!
Milli, gib mir ein Bußl!

9 *Ibid.*, p. 72:

Über seine Felder wird der Wagen fahren
und durch seine hohen, stillen Wälder –
ja, zu denen paßt er: hohe stille Wälder;
und dann werden seine Reiter uns entgegenkommen.
'Das ist Eure Herrin', wird er sagen,
'die ich mir geholt hab'', wird er sagen,
'aus der Kaiserstadt, jetzt aber will sie nimmermehr zurück –
bleiben will sie nur bei mir in meinen Wäldern.'

10 *Ibid.*, pp. 79–80:

Mandryka, hören Sie, so wahr ein Gott im Himmel ist,
so haben Sie mir nichts hier zu verzeihen!
Viel eher muß ich Ihnen, wenn ich kann, verzeihen,
was Sie zu mir geredet haben und in welchem Ton!

11 *Ibid.*, p. 89:

Zdenkerl, du bist die Bess're von uns zweien.
Du hast das liebevollere Herz, und nichts ist da für dich,
nichts in der Welt, als was dein Herz dich heißt zu tun.
Ich dank dir schön, du gibst mir eine gute Lehre,
daß wir nichts wollen dürfen, nichts verlangen,
abwägen nicht und markten nicht und geizen nicht,
nur geben und liebhaben immerfort!

Wie sanft du zu mir sprichst! Du bist nicht bös auf mich!
Du bist so unaussprechlich gut, ich kenn' dich, wie dich keiner
    kennt,
und immer möcht' ich alles dir zuliebe tun –
und nur verschwinden hätt' ich mögen still
und euch nicht kränken! Aber du verstehst mich, du,
und wirst mich nicht verlassen, was auch jetzt noch kommt!

12 *Ibid.*, p. 91:

Mit diesem Herrn da trete ich vor Ihnen, hochgeborener Herr,
verneige mich und bitte für ihn als meinen Freund,
daß Sie die Hand nicht weigern ihm von diesem jungen Fräulein.

13 *Ibid.*, p. 93:

> Sie gibt mir keinen Blick, sie sagt nicht gute Nacht,
> sie läßt mich stehn und geht. Hab' ich was anderes verdient?
> Was ist verdient auf dieser Welt? Verdient ist nichts.
> Stockprügel sind verdient für einen Kerl wie mich –
> aber geschenkt hätt' ich gerne einen Blick genommen –
> so einen halben Blick!
>
> Sie hat gar nichts gemeint, als ein Glas Wasser haben
> und Ruh vor meinem Anblick. Oder spotten hat sie wollen.
> Vielleicht – ? Wenn sie nur spottet, wenigstens
> ist's doch schon eine Gnade, eine unverdiente, das weiß Gott!

14 *Ibid.*, p. 94:

> Das war sehr gut, Mandryka, daß Sie noch nicht fortgegangen
>   sind –
> das Glas da hab' ich austrinken wollen ganz allein
> auf das Vergessen von dem Bösen, was gewesen ist,
> und still zu Bette gehn und nicht denken mehr an Sie und mich,
> bis wieder heller Tag gekommen wäre über uns.
> Dann aber, wie ich Sie gespürt hab' hier im Finstern stehn,
> hat eine große Macht mich angerührt von oben bis ans Herz,
> daß ich mich nicht erfrischen muß mit einem Trunk:
> nein, mich erfrischt schon das Gefühl von meinem Glück,
> und diesen unberührten Trunk kredenz' ich meinen Freund
> den Abend, wo die Mädchenzeit zu Ende ist für mich.

15 *Ibid.*, p. 95:

> So wahr aus diesem Glas da keiner trinken wird nach mir,
> so bist du mein und ich bin dein auf ewige Zeit!

3 The literary sources of the opera

1 The original *Briefwechsel* was published in 1925 by the collaborators themselves, and incorporated a selection of the letters written between 1907 and 1918. This edition appeared in English in 1928. A German revision published in 1952 undertaken by Franz and Alice Strauss together with Willi Schuh included all the then known letters and this was brought up to date in the reprint of 1955. The English translation by Hammelmann and Osers appeared in 1961. There is no doubt that the publication in English has contributed to the reappraisal of the operas, and especially to our sense of the conscious collaboration of two masters.

2 'Danaë oder die Vernunftheirat', see *Correspondence*, 1920, pp. 333–8. The sketches Hofmannsthal supplied ultimately contributed to Joseph Gregor's *Die Liebe der Danaë*, written for Strauss between 1936 and 1938.

3 *Correspondence*, September 1916 (S), p. 262

4 At this point the collaboration directed its energies towards an adapta-

tion for the Vienna Staatsoper of Beethoven's *Prometheus* and *Die Ruinen von Athen* as a ballet spectacular.

5 *Correspondence*, 18 September 1919 (H), p. 331
6 *Der Schwierige* (1921) and *Der Unbestechliche* (1923)
7 *Correspondence*, 23 June 1912 (H), p. 133
8 Hofmannsthal, *Lucidor, Neue Freie Presse*, Vienna (September 1910)
9 *Correspondence*, 8 September 1923 (S), p. 364
10 *Ibid.*, 8 November 1924 (H), p. 394
11 Hofmannsthal to Max Pirker, 15 June 1924, quoted in Hans Albrecht Koch (ed.), *Hugo von Hofmannsthal, Sämtliche Werke* (30 vols., Fischer, Frankfurt, 1975ff), vol. 26, *Operndichtungen 4*
12 Max Pirker, *Teutsche Arien, welche auf dem Keyserlich-privilegirten wienerischen Theatro in unterschiedlich producirten Comodien, deren Titul hier jedes mahl beygerucket gesungen worden* (Vienna, 1927)
13 Adolph Bäuerle, *Komisches Theater*, vol. 3, 1821
14 Hofmannsthal to Joseph Gregor, 17 November 1924, quoted in Koch (ed.), *Hofmannsthal, Werke*, vol. 26, *Operndichtungen 4*
15 Strauss was appointed joint director (with Franz Schalk) of the Vienna Staatsoper in 1919, resigning after a disagreement with his colleague in 1924.
16 *Correspondence*, 1 October 1927 (H), p. 442
17 Other influences noted in Hofmannsthal's sketches include *Die Fledermaus*, and Heuberger's *Opernball* (ballroom scene), Wieland's *Novelle ohne Titel*, Ben Jonson's *Volpone* (the rich uncle), Massinger's *A New Way to Pay Old Debts* (Sir Giles Overreach (Waldner's sacrifice of his daughter to a rich suitor)) and Stendhal's *Le Rouge et Le Noir*.
18 Richard Strauss and Ludwig Karpath, *Briefwechsel*, 17 September 1928, 17 October 1928 and 19 October 1928, in *Richard Strauss-Blätter der Internationalen Richard Strauss-Gesellschaft* 7 (1976), p. 6
19 Alfred Pick, quoted in Vienna Staatsoper programme for *Arabella*, 1 March 1983, p. 9
20 Friedrich Schlögl, *Wiener Feuilletons* (1876), quoted in Koch (ed.), *Hofmannsthal, Werke*, vol. 26, *Operndichtungen 4*
21 The film version was for the actor Gustav Waldau, who had created the rôle of Hans Karl Bühl in *Der Schwierige* in 1921.
22 *Correspondence*, 30 June 1927 (S), pp. 431ff
23 *Ibid.*, 16 July 1927 (H), p. 438
24 *Ibid.*, 20 September 1927 (S), p. 439
25 *Ibid.*, 1 October 1927 (H), p. 442
26 *Ibid.*, 13 November 1927 (H), p. 454
27 *Ibid.*, 5 December 1927 (H), p. 455
28 *Ibid.*, 20 November 1927 (H), p. 455

4 The *Arabella* collaboration

1 *Correspondence*, 13 November 1927 (H), p. 454
2 *Ibid.*, 5 December 1927 (H), p. 455
3 R. A. Schröder and Arthur Schnitzler, 'Briefe', in *Die Neue Rundschau*, 65 (1954), pp. 383–400

4 *Correspondence*, 5 December 1927 (H), p. 455
5 A = *Dramatis Personae, Spieloper* version. B = Hofmannsthal's revised
list for the amalgamated *Fiaker/Lucidor* project. Quoted in Hans
Albrecht Koch (ed.), *Hugo von Hofmannsthal, Sämtliche Werke* (30 vols.,
Fischer, Frankfurt, 1975ff), vol. 26, *Operndichtungen 4*

A	B
Eugen ⎫	Wladimir, Conte Waldner
Lamoral ⎬ Grafen	Die Gräfin seine Gattin geb. Rzewinska
Dominik ⎭	Arabella
Matteo ein Leutenant	Lucile
Nazi	Matteo
Der Pinogl ⎫	Hannibal
Der Ungar Schackerl ⎬ Fiaker	Fiaker (3)
Der Weissfisch ⎭	Herr v. Ürmening ein reicher Gutsbesitzer
Der Fuxmundihansel	Hotelier
Der Sandor	Stubenmädchen
Mandryka (ohne weitere Namen)	'Der Fiakergraf'

6 *Correspondence*, 18 December 1927 (S), p. 458
7 *Correspondence*, 22 December 1927 (H), pp. 460–1
8 *Ibid.*, p. 459
9 *Ibid.*, p. 460
10 *Ibid.*
11 *Correspondence*, 21 December 1927 (S), p. 459
12 *Correspondence*, 22 December 1927 (H), p. 463
13 *Correspondence*, 25 December 1927 (H), p. 465
14 *Ibid.*, p. 466
15 Willi Schuh, 'Zur ursprünglichen Fassung des ersten Aktes *Arabella*',
Die Neue Rundschau, 65 (1954)
16 *Correspondence*, 3 May 1928 (S), p. 475
17 See Koch (ed.) *Hofmannsthal, Werke*, vol. 26, *Operndichtungen 4*,
pp. 95–6.
18 See *Arabella oder Der Fiakerball, frühere Fassung*, in H. Steiner (ed.),
Hugo von Hofmannsthal, Gesammelte Werke (14 vols., Fischer, Frankfurt, 1945–59), *Lustspiele 4*, pp. 472–6.
19 *Correspondence*, 20 July 1928 (S), p. 489
20 *Correspondence*, 23 July 1928 (S), p. 490
21 *Correspondence*, 5 August 1928 (H), p. 502
22 Willi Schuh, 'Eine nichtkomponierte Szene zur "Arabella" *Schweizerische Musikzeitung*, 84 (1944), pp. 231–5
23 *Correspondence*, 9 July 1909 (S), pp. 36–9
24 Koch (ed.), *Hofmannsthal, Werke*, vol. 26, *Operndichtungen 4*
25 *Correspondence*, 13 August 1928 (H), p. 505
26 *Correspondence*, 8 August 1928 (S), pp. 502–3
27 Jankel: one of Mandryka's servants. A Jew, he was to have spied for his
master in the Matteo/Zdenka affair. The collaborators eventually discarded this idea after noting a similarity with the Valzacchi/Annina
theme of *Der Rosenkavalier*.

28 *Correspondence*, 11 August 1928 (H), p. 504
29 29 December 1928
30 *Correspondence*, 3 May 1928 (S), p. 475
31 *Correspondence*, 2 July 1929 (H), p. 533
32 *Ibid.*
33 *Ibid.*, p. 532
34 *Correspondence*, 6 July 1929 (S), p. 534
35 *Correspondence*, 10 July 1929 (H), p. 534
36 *Correspondence*, 14 July 1929 (S), p. 536
37 *Correspondence*, 27 June 1928 (H), p. 482
38 *Correspondence*, 16 July 1929 (S), p. 537
39 *Ibid.*
40 Richard Strauss and Anton Kippenberg, *Briefwechsel*, in *Richard Strauss Jahrbuch*, ed. Willi Schuh (Boosey & Hawkes, London, 1959/60), p. 116

5 The structure of the opera

1 *Correspondence*, 22 December 1912 (H), p. 151
2 *Ibid.*, 21 June 1928 (H), p. 481
3 *Ibid.*, 9 May 1928 (S), p. 478
4 *Ibid.*, 27 June 1928 (H), p. 483
5 *Ibid.*, 9 May 1928 (S), p. 477
6 *Ibid.*, 13 July 1928 (H), p. 485
7 *Ibid.*, 3 May 1928 (S), p. 275
8 *Ibid.*, 24 June 1928 (S), p. 481
9 *Ibid.*, 8 August 1928 (S), p. 504

6 Analysis: technique and expression

1 *Correspondence*, 18 December 1911 (H), p. 108
2 *Ibid.*, pp. 108–9
3 Ronald Peacock, *The Poet in the Theatre* (MacGibbon & Kee, London, 1961), p. 142
4 *Ibid.*, p. 136
5 *Ibid.*, p. 142

7 The Act 3 sketchbook

1 Wagner heard *Lohengrin* for the first time on 15 May 1861, although the Viennese premiere was in 1858. Both performances took place in the old Kärntnertortheater, the Oper am Ring not being opened until 1869.
2 See Norman Del Mar, *Richard Strauss*, 2 vols. (Barrie and Rockliff, London, 1969), vol. 2, pp. 405 and 411.
3 Stefan Zweig, *The World of Yesterday* (Cassell, London, 1943), p. 279

8 Premiere and aftermath

1 Strauss's average composition-time for an opera works out at just over two years for each. Taking the multi-act works alone, the average in-

creases to just short of three years. *Arabella* occupied Strauss for three
years and three months from start to finish, *Die ägyptische Helena* just
four years, the *Danaë* slightly more than two years, with *Die Frau ohne
Schatten*, 'interrupted' of course by the outbreak of World War 1, requir-
ing three years and eight months. Against this, on the other hand,
Der Rosenkavalier took just over one, and *Die schweigsame Frau* just
under two years, to reach completion.

2 Baron Clemens von Frankenstein (1875–1942), German composer, was
   Intendant of the Munich Opera from 1912 to 1918, and again from 1924
   to 1934.
3 Alfred Mathis, 'Elisabeth Schumann', *Opera*, 25/1 (1974), p. 28
4 Richard Strauss to Clemens Krauss, unpublished, 16 August 1929,
   Musiksammlung, Österreichische Nationalbibliothek, Vienna
5 Richard Strauss and Ludwig Karpath, *Briefwechsel*, 21 September
   1929, in *Richard Strauss-Blätter der Internationalen Richard Strauss-
   Gesellschaft*, 7 (May 1976), p. 8
6 Strauss to Krauss, *Briefwechsel*, 4 June 1929
7 Strauss to Krauss, unpublished, 17 October 1931 Strauss to Karpath, 18
   September 1931; Strauss to Fritz Busch, 23 September 1931, quoted in
   Otto Erhardt, *Richard Strauss – Leben – Werken – Schaffen* (Otto Walter,
   Olten 1953), p. 355
8 Strauss to Krauss
9 Erhardt, *Strauss* p. 355
10 *Ibid.*
11 See Fritz Busch, *Pages from a Musician's Life*, trans. Marjorie Strachey
   (Hogarth Press, London, 1953), pp. 169ff.
12 Heinz Tietjen (1881–1967): German conductor and producer, *Intendant*
   of the Berlin State Opera 1927–45, artistic director at Bayreuth, 1931–44.
   A long-standing colleague of Strauss, who dedicated *Die Liebe der Danaë*
   to him.
13 Busch, *Pages*
14 Strauss to Krauss, 27 March 1933
15 *Ibid.*
16 Richard Strauss to Leonhard Fanto, unpublished, 4 April 1933, *Musiksammlung*, Österreichische Nationalbibliothek, Vienna
17 Strauss to Krauss, 10 April 1933
18 Strauss to Krauss, 20 April 1933
19 Dr Anton Kippenberg (1874–1950), director of the Insel Verlag. As a
   close friend of Strauss he was responsible for initiating the collaborative
   link between the composer and Stefan Zweig which resulted in *Die
   schweigsame Frau*.
20 Richard Strauss and Anton Kippenberg, *Briefwechsel*, 29 March 1933, in
   Richard Strauss Jahrbuch 1959/60, p. 120
21 Krauss and Ursuleac were married after the Second World War.
22 The sketch book for the *Arabella* Act 3 *finale* was presented to Kutzschbach, inscribed 'To my dear colleague opera director Hermann Kutzschbach on the occasion of the 40th Dresden Arabella, with sincerest greetings Dr Richard Strauss'
23 Josef Gielen (1890–1968) was brought into opera by Busch from the

straight theatre. Subsequently, in 1935, after the Dresden *Arabella*, he produced *Der Rosenkavalier* in Berlin for Krauss, who thought highly of him. After the war he became director of the Burgtheater in Vienna.

24 Viorica Ursuleac: see Roswitha Schlötterer, *Singen für Richard Strauss* (Doblinger, Vienna, 1986), p. 15.
25 *Das schöne Sachsen* (Dresden 1933), pp. 162–3
26 Strauss to Karpath, 9 July 1933, p. 14
27 Karpath to Strauss, 4 July 1933, p. 14
28 Dr Lothar Wallerstein (1882–1949). Trained as a medical doctor, became a conductor and eventually an opera producer. He worked closely with Strauss and Krauss in Vienna, where from 1927 until 1938 he held a post at the Staatsoper.
29 *Neues Wiener Journal*, 22 October 1933, p. 3
30 Lotte Lehmann, *Singing with Richard Strauss* (Hamish Hamilton, London, 1964), p. 85
31 The first performance of *Arabella* at the Paris Opéra took place in April 1981! Production: Hartleb; Decor: Rice; Te Kanawa (Ar); Aruhn (Z); Grundheber (M) and Böhme (W)
32 Rudolph Hartmann, *Richard Strauss: The Staging of his Operas and Ballets* (Phaidon, Oxford, 1981) p. 187
33 Dr Götz-Klaus Kende, letter to the author, 23 September 1987
34 I am indebted to Dr Kende for this information.
35 The published *Briefwechsel* between Strauss and Krauss omits most of the earlier letters, concentrating on those which relate to *Capriccio*. All Strauss communications to Krauss are now located in the *Musiksammlung* of the Österreichische Nationalbibliothek in Vienna.
36 Strauss to Krauss, *Briefwechsel*, 17 July 1942, p. 256
37 *Ibid.*, p. 258
38 *Ibid.*, p. 257
39 *Ibid.*, 25 March 1942, p. 242
40 The Berlin, Dresden, Munich and Vienna opera houses had all been destroyed by Allied bombing.
41 Dr K. H. in *Demokratisches Volksblatt*, Salzburg, 31 July 1958
42 *Die Presse*, Vienna, 8 November 1977
43 The recent Tate/Te Kanawa recording by Decca – issued late 1987 – is also uncut (see Discography, p. 157).
44 *Opern Welt*, March 1987, pp. 23–4
45 Hartmann, *The Staging*, pp. 177–93

9 Critical reaction

1 Neville Cardus, *Talking of Music* (Collins, London, 1957), p. 96
2 *The Sunday Times*, 20 September 1953
3 Stefan Zweig to Richard Strauss, 17 May 1934, in *Briefwechsel*, ed. Willi Schuh (Fischer, Frankfurt, 1957), pp. 61–2
4 *The Times*, Friday 13 May 1934, p. 12
5 *The Times*, Wednesday 16 September 1953 p. 3
6 *The Guardian*, Wednesday 16 September 1953

7 *Neues Österreich*, Vienna, 12 June 1952, p. 6
8 Joseph Gregor, Vienna Staatsoper programme, 21 October 1933, pp. 11–12
9 *Schweizerische Musikzeitung und Sängerblatt*, 73 (1933), p. 536
10 *Neues Wiener Journal*, 22 October 1933, p. 3
11 *A Zene (Musik)*, 16/9, Budapest, 15 January 1935. In view of his subsequent relationship to this opera, it is interesting to note that Sir Georg Solti was employed at the Hungarian State Opera as repetiteur up to 1938. It seems likely that his first impressions of *Arabella* would have stemmed from rehearsals of this production.
12 Richard Strauss and Hugo von Hofmannsthal, *Briefwechsel*, ed. F. and A. Strauss (Atlantis, Zurich, 1952)
13 *The Daily Telegraph*, 13 September 1953
14 Georg Marek, *Richard Strauss: The Life of a Non-Hero* (Gollancz, London, 1967), p. 267
15 William Mann, 'Champion of Strauss', *Opera*, December 1984
16 Gerhard Brunner, *Illustrierte Kronen Zeitung*, Vienna, 4 May 1969
17 Franz Endler, *Die Presse*, Vienna, 5 May 1969
18 Willi Schuh, *Über Opern von Richard Strauss* (Atlantis, Zurich, 1947), pp. 55–6
19 *Ibid.*, p. 60
20 Mann, 'Champion'
21 Philip Hope-Wallace, *The Gramophone*, March 1958, p. 418
22 Edward Greenfield, *The Gramophone*, June 1964, p. 18
23 Olin Downes, *The New York Times*, 11 February 1955
24 Norman Del Mar, *Richard Strauss*, 2 vols. (Barrie and Rockliff, London, 1969), vol. 2, p. 437
25 Michael Kennedy, *The Daily Telegraph*, August 1984

10 An interpretative assessment

1 A play-reading of *Der Rosenkavalier* took place in the *Schloßtheater* at Schönbrunn, Vienna on 4 June 1961, directed by Rudolf Steinbock.
2 Quoted in Ronald Peacock, *The Poet in the Theatre* (MacGibbon & Kee, London, 1961); see Chapter 1, p. 3.
3 *Correspondence*, 5 August 1928 (H), p. 501
4 *Ibid.*, 26 July 1928 (H), p. 460
5 *Ibid.*, 30 April 1928 (H), p. 473
6 *Ibid.*, 23 July 1928 (S), p. 490
7 *Ibid.*, 5 August 1928 (H), p. 501
8 See *Arabella* libretto, p. 89, lines 1–7. For German text and translation see Chapter 2, note 11.
9 Viewed in its historical context and taking into consideration the general pattern of Hofmannsthal's achievement, one is forced to conclude that below the surface of this simple tale of a young girl's emergence to womanhood, deeper implications lie. It is a mark of Hofmannsthal's stature, as well as a consequence of the symbolism that he had so consistently employed from his earliest years, that his work acquires an inter-

pretative universality all too easy to abuse. It is scarcely out of place, however, given his acknowledged patriotism, and writing as he was in the shadow of *Der Turm*, for him to have subconsciously created, in this late-1920s *Arabella*, an allegory of the spiritual resurgence of his homeland. On behalf of a country drained by war, stripped of power and shorn of past territorial glories, he constantly sought renewal of that unique 'Austrianism' in which he so passionately believed. The Arabella/ Mandryka embrace might well, even unconsiously, symbolise such a renewal – 'You will never change, will you?' he implores at the end of the opera; 'Indeed, I cannot', she replies, 'Take me as I am.' Thus, the immutability of her being, and the preservation of the quintessential Austrian spirit, is confirmed.

10 *Correspondence*, 26 July 1928 (H), p. 496
11 Stefan Zweig, *The World of Yesterday* (Cassell, London, 1943) p. 279
12 William Mann, *Richard Strauss: A Critical Study of the Operas* (Cassell, London, 1964), p. 269
13 *Ibid.*
14 *Correspondence*, 10 July 1929 (H), p. 534
15 Mann, *A Critical Study*, p. 269

Select bibliography

Published source documents

Bäuerle, Adolf, *Komisches Theater*, Budapest, 1820–26.
Hofmannsthal, Hugo von, *Gesammelte Werke*, ed. H. Steiner, 14 vols.,
  Fischer, Frankfurt, 1947–59. *Die Erzählungen*, 1953.
  Lustspiele 2, 1948.
  Lustspiele 4, 1956.
  Sämtliche Werke ed. Hans Albrecht Koch, 30 vols., Fischer, Frankfurt,
  1975–. Vol. 26, *Operndichtungen 4*, 1976.
Schuh, Willi, *Straussiana aus vier Jahrzehnten*, Hans Schneider, Tutzing,
  1981.
Schuh, Willi, 'Eine nichtkomponierte Szene zur "Arabella"', *Schweizerische
  Musikzeitung*, 84 (1944).
Trenner, Franz, *Die Skizzenbücher von Richard Strauss*, Hans Schneider,
  Tutzing, 1977.

Published collections of letters

Strauss, R., and Hofmannsthal, H. von, *Briefwechsel*, ed. F. and A. Strauss,
  Atlantis, Zurich, 1952.
  Briefwechsel, ed. Willi Schuh, Atlantis, Zurich, 1964–70.
  Correspondence, trans. H. Hammelmann and E. Osers, Collins, London,
  1961.
Strauss, R., and Karpath, L., *Briefwechsel* ed. Günter Brosche, *Richard
  Strauss-Blätter der Internationalen Richard Strauss-Gesellschaft*, 7,
  (1976), pp. 1–14.
Strauss, R., and Kippenberg, A., *Briefwechsel*, in *Richard Strauss Jahrbuch*,
  ed. Willi Schuh, Boosey & Hawkes, London, 1959/60.
Strauss, R., and Krauss, C., *Briefwechsel*, ed. Götz Klaus Kende and Willi
  Schuh, C. H. Beck, Munich, 1964.
Strauss, R., and Schuh, W. *Briefwechsel*, Atlantis, Zurich, 1969.
Strauss, R., and Zweig, S., *Briefwechsel*, ed. Willi Schuh, Fischer, Frankfurt
  1957.
  A Confidential Matter: Letters of R. Strauss and S. Zweig 1931–35, trans.
  Max Knight, University of California Press, 1977.

154   *Select bibliography*

Richard Strauss, *Betrachtungen und Erinnerungen*, ed. Willi Schuh, Atlantis, Zurich, 1949.
Bibliographie, vol. 1, ed. Franz Grasberger, Prachner, Vienna, 1964.
Bibliographie, vol. 2, ed. Günter Brosche, Brüder Hollinek, Vienna, 1973.

Unpublished documents

Richard Strauss letters to Karl Böhm, Vienna Philharmonic Archive.
Letters to Clemens Krauss, Österreichische Nationalbibliothek, *Musiksammlung* 34.244, Clemens Krauss Archive
Letter to L. Fanto, 7 April 1933, Österreichische Nationalbibliothek, *Musiksammlung* 34.244, Clemens Krauss Archive.
Revision of Fiakermilli song (full score and vocal score; Act 2, Fig. 42–43), Österreichische Nationalbibliothek, *Musiksammlung* 34.244, Clemens Krauss Archive.
Arabella sketch book (Act 3), Österreichische Nationalbibliothek, *Musiksammlung* 34.244, Clemens Krauss Archive.

Published Arabella texts and translations

Libretto, Adolph Fürstner, Berlin 1933 (German).
In Hofmannsthal, Hugo von, *Gesammelte Werke*, ed. H. Steiner, 15 vols., Fischer, Frankfurt, 1947–59, *Lustspiele 4*.
In Hofmannsthal, Hugo von, *Selected Plays and Libretti* ed. Michael Hamburger, trans. Nora Wydenbruck and Christopher Middleton, Routledge & Kegan Paul, London, 1964.
In English National Opera Guide No. 30, *Arabella* trans. John Gutman (with cuts), Calder, London, 1985, pp. 53–110.
RM Arts in association with Glyndebourne Productions Ltd., trans. John Gutman (with cuts), 1984.
Decca textbook, trans. Chris Wood, 1987.

Scores

Full score, Adolph Fürstner, Berlin, 1933; Boosey & Hawkes, London.
Vocal score, Adolph Fürstner, Berlin, 1933; Boosey & Hawkes, London.
Study score, Boosey & Hawkes, London, 1960.

Guides

English National Opera, Guide No. 30, *Arabella*, Calder, London, 1985.
See articles, essays, etc. published by Decca (1957), Deutsche Grammophon (1963), EMI (1981).

Books

Abert, Anna, Amalie, *Richard Strauss: Drei Opern*, Friedrich Verlag, Welber, 1972.
Busch, Fritz, *Pages from a Musician's Life*, trans. Marjorie Strachey, Hogarth Press, London, 1953.

Cardus, Neville, *Talking of Music*, Collins, London, 1957.

Del Mar, Norman, *Richard Strauss*, 3 vols., Barrie and Rockliff, London, 1969.

Deppisch, Walter, *Richard Strauss*, Rowohlt, Reinbeck bei Hamburg, 1968.

Erhardt, Otto, *Richard Strauss – Leben – Werken – Schaffen*, Otto Walter, A. G. Olten, 1953.

Gregor, Joseph, *Clemens Krauss: Seine musikalische Sendung*, Walter Krieg, Vienna, 1953.

Geschichte des österreichischen Theaters, Donau Verlag, Vienna, 1948.

Richard Strauss, der Meister der Oper, 2nd edn, Piper, Munich, 1943.

Hartmann, Rudolf, *Richard Strauss: The Staging of his Operas and Ballets*, Phaidon, Oxford, 1981.

Jefferson, Alan, *The Operas of Richard Strauss in Britain (1910–1963)*, Putnam, London, 1963.

'Richard Strauss' Operas Performed in Great Britain (1910–1985)' in *Richard Strauss-Blätter der Internationalen Richard-Strauss-Gesellschaft*, 7 (1986), pp. 104–79.

Keith-Smith, Brian, 'Hugo von Hofmannsthal', in *German Men of Letters*, ed. Alex Natan, 2 vols., Oswald Wolff, London, 1961.

Kende, Götz Klaus, *Clemens Krauss als Direktor der Wiener Staatsoper*, Residenz Verlag, Salzburg, 1971.

Kennedy, Michael, *Richard Strauss*, Master Musicians, Dent, London, 1976.

Kralik, Heinrich, *Richard Strauss, Weltbürger der Musik*, Wollzeilen Verlag, Vienna, 1963.

Krause, Ernst, *Richard Strauss: Gestalt und Werke*, Breitkopf & Härtel, Leipzig, 1963; trans. John Coombs, as *Richard Strauss*, Collet's, London, 1964.

Lehmann, Lotte, *Singing with Richard Strauss*, Hamish Hamilton, London, 1964.

Marek, George, *Richard Strauss: The Life of a Non-Hero*, Gollancz, London, 1967.

Mann, William, *Richard Strauss: A Critical Study of the Operas*, Cassell, London, 1964.

Obermayer, August, and Herd, E. W. (ed.), *A Glossary of German Literary Terms*, University of Otago, New Zealand, 1983.

Peacock, Ronald, *The Poet in the Theatre*, MacGibbon & Kee, London, 1961.

Prawy, Marcel, *Die Wiener Oper*, Verlag Fritz Molden, Vienna, 1969.

Schäfer, Rudolph, *Hugo von Hofmannsthal's 'Arabella'*, Herbert Lang, Berne, 1967.

Schlötterer, Roswitha, *Singen für Richard Strauss*, Doblinger, Vienna, 1986.

Schuh, Willi, *Über Opern von Richard Strauss*, Atlantis, Zurich, 1947.

Trenner, Franz, *Richard Strauss: Dokumente seines Lebens und Schaffens*, C. H. Beck, Munich, 1954.

Ursuleac, Viorica, 'Meine Erinnerungen an Richard Strauss', in Schlötterer, Roswitha, *Singen für Richard Strauss*, Doblinger, Vienna, 1986, pp. 7–23.

Volke, Werner, *Hofmannsthal*, Rowohlt, Reinbeck bei Hamburg, 1967.

Discography

Ar: Arabella, Z: Zdenka, Ad: Adelaide, Wa: Waldner, M: Mandryka, Mat: Matteo, E: Elemer, Do: Dominik, La: Lamoral, Fm: Fiakermilli, Ft: Fortune-teller.
All recordings are in stereo unless otherwise stated.
* denotes mono recording; (c) denotes cassette; (cd) denotes compact disc.

Complete

1947   Böhm/Vienna State Opera Chorus/Vienna Philharmonic Orchestra (live)
Reining (Ar); Della Casa (Z); Anday (Ad); Hann (Wa); Hotter (M); Taubmann (Mat); Patzak (E); Witt (Do); Poell (La); Handl (Fm); Michaelis (Ft). (Combines Acts 2 and 3)
Discocorp (Bruno Walter Society)
MELODRAM MEL S 101*

1957   Solti/Vienna State Opera Chorus/Vienna Philharmonic Orchestra
Della Casa (Ar); Güden (Z); Malaniuk (Ad); Edelmann (Wa); London (M); Dermota (Mat); Kmentt (E); Wächter (Do); Pröglhof (La); Coertse (Fm); Hellwig (Ft)
Decca 635104 EK (B)

1963   Keilberth/Bavarian State Opera Chorus and Orchestra (live)
Della Casa (Ar); Rothenberger (Z); Malaniuk (Ad.) Kohn (Wa); Fischer-Dieskau (M); Paskuda (Mat); Uhl (E); Hoppe (Do); Günter (La); Rogner (Fm) Reich (Ft). (combines Acts 2 and 3)
DG 2721 163 (B); (c) 415 384/4

1973   Rennert (W)/Italian Radio Orchestra and chorus (live)
Caballé (Ar); Miljakovic (Z); Dominguez (Ad); Moll (Wa); Nimsgern (M); Kollo (Ma); Giafa (E); Borgato (Do); Monreale (La); Scavotti (Fm); Falcone (Ft)
Her 404*

1981   Sawallisch/Bavarian State Opera Chorus and Orchestra
Varady (Ar); Donath (Z); Schmidt (Ad); Berry (Wa); Fischer-Dieskau (M); Dallapozza (Mat); Winkler (E); Küper (Do); Becht (La); Höbarth (Fm) Soffel (Ft). (Combines Acts 2 and 3)
EMI 165–64456/58 (b) SLS 5224 (Digital)

1984   Haitink/Glyndebourne Festival Chorus/London Philharmonic Orchestra (live)

156

Putnam (Ar); Rolandi (Z); Sarfaty (Ad); Korn (Wa); Bröcheler (M); Lewis (Mat); Winslade (E); Munro (Do); Moses (La); Bradley (Fm); Hartle (Ft)
Video tape recording commercially available
Glyndebourne Productions Ltd. Produced by BBC Television in association with RM Arts. TVT 90 31282

1986   Tate/Orchestra and chorus of the Royal Opera House, Covent Garden
Te Kanawa (Ar); Fontana (Z); Dernesch (Ad); Gutstein (Wa); Grundheber (M); Seiffert (Mat); Ionitza (E); Cachemaille (Do); Rydl (La); Bradley (Fm); Runkel (Ft)

> Decca 6.35751 FX. 8.35751 (3CDS) ZB;
> (*c*) 435 751 FX; (*cd*) 417 623-2 2B

Excerpts

1933   Krauss/Vienna Staatsoper; Ursuleac (Ar); Bokor (Z); Rünger (Ad); Mayr (Wa); Jerger (M); Kern (Fm)
Aber der Richtige; So fließt die helle, stille Donau; Fand ein Mädchen: Teletheater (Belvcdere) 120481*

1933   Krauss/Berlin Staatskapelle; Ursuleac (Ar); Bokor (Z)
Aber der Richtige; So wie sie sind

> *Pol 62712* (ELP 30541)**

Krauss/Berlin Staatskapelle; Ursuleac (Ar); Jerger (M)
Das war sehr gut, Mandryka

> *Pol 62711* DE 7025**

Jäger/Berlin Staatskapelle; Lehmann (Ar); Heidersbach (Z)
Aber der Richtige

> *P RO 20236*; Odeon O-4843*; Seraphim 1C-6041**

Jäger/Berlin Staatskapelle; Lehmann (Ar)
Mein Elemer

> *EMI DACAPO 1C 137–30 705 M* (Odeon 0–4842*)*
> *Seraphim 1C–6041**

Zaun/Berlin Staatskapelle
Interlude; Waltz and Staircase music

> *HMV B 8175* EG 3031* Vic 4282**

1934   Reuss/Berlin Philharmonic; Fuchs (Ar); Wieber (Z); Schöffler (M)
Aber der Richtige; Und du wirst mein Gebieter sein

> *Telef E 1477 Acanta KB 22179**

1940   Seidler-Winkler/Berlin Staatskapelle; Lemnitz (Ar); Hüsch (M)
Mein Elemer; So wie sie sind; Und du wirst mein Gebieter sein

> *EMI DACAPO 1C 147–28 990 M* (DB 5606*)*

1943   Gruber/Berlin Staatskapelle; Lemnitz (Ar); Hüsch (M)
Das war sehr gut, Mandryka

> *ACANTA MA 22110**

1943   Böhm/Dresden Staatskapelle; Teschemacher (Ar); Goltz (Z); Ahlersmeyer (M)
Das war sehr gut, Mandryka; Aber der Richtige; Du wirst mein Gebieter sein; Sie gibt mir keinen Blick

> *ACANTA 40 23 280**

Böhm/Dresden Staatskapelle; Teschemacher (Ar); Beilke (Z)
Er ist der Richtige nicht; Das war sehr gut, Mandryka
DB 4675*
1954   Von Matacic/Philharmonia Orchestra; Schwarzkopf (Ar); Felber-
mayer (Z); Schlott (Wa); Metternich (M); Gedda (Mat); Dickie (E);
Pröglhoff (Do); Berry (La)
*Ich danke Fräulein; Aber der Richtige; Welko das Bild!; Mein
Elemer; Sie wollen mich heiraten; Und du wirst mein Gebieter sein;
Und jetzt sag ich Adieu; Das war sehr gut, Mandryka*
EMI ANGEL 35194*
1957   Solti/Vienna Philharmonic Orchestra; Della Casa (Ar); Güden
(Z); London (M)
Er ist der Richtige nicht für mich; Das war sehr gut, Mandryka
CEP 612 ST SEP 5031
1958   Schüchter/Philharmonia Orchestra; Rysanek (Ar)
Das war sehr gut, Mandryka
EMI DACAPO 1C 147–29 151 M (LX 1559)
1966   Neuhaus/Dresden Staatskapelle; Della Casa (Ar); Rothenberger (Z)
Die schönen Rosen!; Aber der Richtige
SME 80 999 CSDW 7382
1972   Weller/Vienna Philharmonic Orchestra; Lorengar (Ar); Auger (Z)
Ich danke Fräulein; Aber der Richtige
DECCA: SXL 6525
1981   Sawallisch/Bayerisches Staatsorchester; Varady (Ar); Donath (Z);
Schmidt (Ad); Berry (Wa); Fischer-Dieskau (M); Dallapozza
(Mat); Winkler (E); Küper (Do); Höbarth (Fm)
(Act 1) *Die schönen Rosen – Aber der Richtige; Was hast du denn
– Heute ist mein Tag!; Herr Graf, Sie haben Ihrem werten Brief;
Mein Elemer*
(Act 2) *Sie wollen mich heiraten – Und du wirst mein Gebieter sein
– Die Wiener Herr'n versteh'n sich*
(Act 3) *Ich komme Heim vom Ball; Sehr gut, Jetzt habe ich mein
richtiges Vis-à-Vis; Das war sehr gut, Mandryka*
EMI HMV 1C O61 1650601/4
1984   Kuhn/Kölner Rundfunk Orchester; Rothenberger (Ar); Brink-
mann (M)
Und du wirst mein Gebieter sein
EMI 1C 246y 14 6824 4
1988   Stein/Bamberger Symphoniker: Popp (Ar); Titus (M)
(Act 1) *Mein Elemer*; (Act 2) *Und du wirst mein Gebieter sein*;
(Act 3) Finale from *Das war sehr gut, Mandryka . . .*
ARIOLA 208 938. Compact Disc 258938

Other broadcast recordings

*Tape recordings of five complete Arabella broadcasts were made by, and are
held in, the* British Library National Sound Archive. *Since these perfor-*

mances are available, by appointment, to the listening public, details are (by permission of the archive) supplied below.

1965   Solti/Covent Garden Orchestra and Chorus
Della Casa (Ar); Carlyle (Z); Veasey (Ad); Langdon (Wa); Fischer-Dieskau (M); Young (Mat); Macdonald (E); Bryne Jones (Do); Godfrey (La); Eddy (Fm); Pierce (Ft)
Broadcast 6 February 1965. 753–6 W/P 119 R

1979   Solti/Vienna Philharmonic
Janowitz (Ar); Ghazarian (Z); Lilowa (Ad); Krämer (Wa); Weikl (M); Kollo (Mat); Frannsson (E); Helm (Do); Rudi (La); Gruberova (Fm); Mödl (Ft)
Broadcast 3 November 1979. T2634BW/T2635BW/T2636BW

1980   Elder/English National Opera Orchestra and Chorus (English translation)
Barstow (Ar); Burrows (Z); Squires (Ad); Blackburn (Wa); Glossop (M); Clark (Mat); Howell (E); Kitchiner (Do); Earle (La); Hill Smith (Fm); Bostock (Ft)
Broadcast 11 November 1980. T3479BW/T3483BW/T3484BW

1981   Pritchard/Orchestra and Chorus of the Royal Opera House, Covent Garden
Te Kanawa (Ar); Ghazarian (Z); Veasey (Ad); Jungwirth (Wa); Wixell (M); O'Neill (Mat); Leggate (E); Gelling (Do); Earle (La); Watson (Fm); Cannan (Ft)
Broadcast 19 October 1981. T4495BW/4496BW/4497BW

1984   Haitink/London Philharmonic Orchestra/Glyndebourne Festival Chorus
Putnam (Ar); Rolandi (Z); Sarfaty (Ad); Korn (Wa); Bröcheler (M); Lewis (Mat); Winslade (E); Munro (Do); Moses (La); Bradley (Fm); Hartle (Ft)
(Simultaneous broadcast with BBC television 12 January 1984).
T7419BW/T7420BW/T7421BW

A recording of highlights from the Viennese premiere of October 1933 was made at rehearsal and broadcast prior to the performance (on 18 October) during the course of a lecture on the work by the producer, Lothar Wallerstein. This comprised three excerpts, presumably including the two duets. It is no longer in existence. (See Günter Lesuig in *Richard Strauss-Blätter der Internationalen Richard Strauss-Gesellschaft*, 9 (1983), p. 77. The East German radio archive still possesses a complete recording of the Salzburg Festival *Arabella* of August 1942 conducted by Clemens Krauss and with Ursuleac in the title role. It is the more unfortunate that this is not generally available, since it doubtless includes the new Fiakermilli arrangements which Strauss supplied to Krauss for this occasion. (I am indebted to Dr Götz-Klaus Kende for this information.)

Index